D1645877

TIPS FOR ACTORS

FERGUS CRAIG

Tips for Actors

FOREWORD BY ELLEN PAGE

OBERON BOOKS
LONDON

WWW.OBERONBOOKS.COM

First published in 2014 by Oberon Books Ltd
521 Caledonian Road, London N7 9RH
Tel: +44 (0) 20 7607 3637 / Fax: +44 (0) 20 7607 3629
e-mail: info@oberonbooks.com
www.oberonbooks.com

A catalogue record for this book is available from the
British Library.

PB ISBN: 978-1-78319-118-5
E ISBN: 978-1-78319-617-3

Cover design by James Illman

Printed, bound and converted
by CPI Group (UK) Ltd, Croydon, CR0 4YY.

Visit www.oberonbooks.com to read more about all our
books and to buy them. You will also find features, author
interviews and news of any author events, and you can
sign up for e-newsletters so that you're always first to hear
about our new releases.

Dedicated to those who have died
in the pursuit of a good acting performance

CONTENTS

FOREWORD

Dear Reader,

I am sure I had the same response as you when you first heard about this book. Intrigue, excitement and gratitude to finally have a concentrated and stripped-down piece of work that could give actors young and old, new and experienced, some thoughts, advice and ultimately, be an encouraging force in a very competitive profession.

The author, a few months ago, had his publisher send me this 'book' that is in your hands. I was very humbled to be asked to write this foreword and opened it right away to read… please, I am begging you, put it down. If you still have the receipt somewhere then you should take it back and get your money returned to you. These 'tips' are ludicrous. Oftentimes they are offensive and I would argue, potentially harmful to not only your career, but you as a person.

Now, could I write a book that offers tips for actors? No. I would not know where to begin. It is a particularly unusual form of art. Intangible moments created with another person that create a separate and hopefully, truthful reality. Finding yourself, while losing yourself. It is an extraordinary experience. All I can really say is, strive to be honest in your work.

My other thought is, stop reading this book right now. This guy does not know what he is talking about. I don't understand how this even made it to print and seeing how clearly brain dead the publisher must be they most likely won't even read what I have written, so I hope I have reached you and warned you.

I am sorry to be the one to disappoint, it would be wonderful to have a collection of wise words that one could use for support. That being said, get used to disappointment, being an actor is mostly disappointment and rejection.

I hope you listen to me. I hope you do not follow this man's counsel.

Ellen Page

NOTE FROM THE AUTHOR

When I was told that Ellen Page had agreed to write a foreword I was delighted. It is only now that I realise that I was getting her mixed up with the legendary musical star Elaine Paige. As for Ellen Page, a quick google search tells me that she's apparently starred in a number of movies.

I really don't have time to read the foreword myself, as I have a reiki session booked in, but I'd like to take this opportunity to sincerely thank her for her support.

INTRODUCTION

Dear Actor,

Firstly I'd like to say thank you. Not for picking up this book – that was inevitable – but for being an actor. Thank you. I think we actors are sometimes so immersed in the day to day nuts and bolts of acting that we forget just how utterly astonishing we are. Yes, what nurses and firefighters and teachers do is fantastic but do we need to hear about it *quite* so much? When a nurse finishes her 'difficult' day at work, what does she do? She turns on the television and watches what? Us. Actors. Once a firefighter has put out a fire, what does he do? He goes to a local studio theatre and watches what? Us. Actors. When a teacher is returning home from an inner-city school who stops her and asks her to give to charity? Us. Out of work actors. It is your backbreaking three-hour days that entertain the world. Thank you.

I have been an actor (on and off) for 25 years and have used my vast experience (Old Vic, Bolton Octagon, four episodes of *Casualty*) to write this guide to acting as a sort of gift[*] to the acting community. Within this book are the tips you need to take your skills and career to the next level. Whether you're a young actor who wants to know how to get started or a more experienced actor who's starting to coast a little – *I'm talking to you Imelda Staunton* – this is the book for you.

---

*   RRP £8.99

I will be delving into every crevice of the acting world to give you a complete manual.[**] Coping with drama school, how to cry on cue, sabotaging your fellow professionals' careers – it's all covered here.

I should mention that the size of the book is deliberate and should not be seen as an indication that the publishers wanted to keep down costs. I have designed it to be carried upon your person at all times for easy reference – perhaps during a taxing audition. Flick through the book and you will also notice that it is littered with helpful pictures and what my son-in-law calls info graphics. This *was* done at the request of my publisher and although I contributed to them I personally think they cheapen the book as a whole.

So tuck in and enjoy! If you're not a better actor by the end of this book then I'll give you your money back guaranteed.[***]

[**]   Should this book sell well I am happy to write a sequel.
[***]   As there is no tangible way of determining this, I will not be giving any refunds.

HOW TO BEHAVE ON YOUR FIRST DAY OF REHEARSALS

The first day of rehearsals is always nerve-wracking. The likelihood is that you won't know many of the cast and you, of course, want to create a good impression. There are a number of ways to do this.

If you're not already a recognisable face in the industry your first concern should be to make sure that everyone knows you're a professional actor to be reckoned with. Always walk in wearing the T-shirt of another production you've been in. This says, loud and clear, 'Think twice before underestimating me. I was in a regional touring production of *Chess*'. They needn't know if you bought it from a charity shop.

Don't rely just on the T-shirt though. You need to keep reminding people that you've worked before. Say things like...

'Oh! A clock! We had one of those in the rehearsal room for *Jonathan Creek* in which I played a police officer for not one but two episodes.'

'How did I get here? On the tube. Which is

TOP TIP!
Every day look in the mirror and shout 10 times...
'I AM AN ACTOR!
I BRING JOY!
I SAVE LIVES!'

funny because that's how I used to get to rehearsals for the *Doll's House* in which I played Servant Number 3 to Colin Firth's Torvald.'

You don't have to be quite as subtle as that though. Here's a nice trick you can try. When the director asks if anyone has any questions before the first read-through put your hand up and say…

'How many credits are we allowed in our programme entries? Because I have twenty-four. Twenty-eight including rehearsed readings'.

The first read-through is very important. There is no getting away from the fact that all of the actors are judging each other on how they perform. If you stumble over a word there is a very real chance that you could be sacked on the spot. In some more brutal, Eastern European theatre companies an actor is often shot for less. This is why I recommend reading as quietly as possible. That way, if you do make a mistake, no one will know. If anyone complains that they can't hear you, shout 'Acting is about listening! You're obviously not listening hard enough!'.

If somebody else messes up then this is a great opportunity to get on the director's side early on by tutting. In fact, tutting is an underused tool by actors throughout the business. If any actor makes a mistake of any kind within a five-mile radius of you, you should always be there with an undermining tut. The worse everyone else is at acting, the better chance you have of getting ahead. Tuts are a superb way of knocking people's confidence and thus diminishing their skills. I am proud to say that I can think of no less than three actors who have given up acting altogether thanks to my persistent tutting. They were deaths by a thousand tuts, if you like. Fewer pro actors means more roles for me. I concede that the fact that they were all women means we weren't in direct competition for roles. You could call it friendly fire. Look, I did what I did. No regrets.

There is likely to come a point in the day where some actors will go for a cigarette. At this stage you will have a difficult choice to make. The movie *Grease* teaches us that smoking (and wearing slutty leather) is cool. Increasingly though scientists are starting to believe that the habit is actually bad for you and more importantly for an actor, bad for your voice. With each production I usually use the first day to suss out which camp I want to fall into. Sometimes I stay indoors and try to win favour with the director by offering him foot rubs. Sometimes I hang with the smokers – damaging my voice but at least staying in touch with company gossip. My favourite solution is to get the best both worlds by standing with the smokers and pretending to smoke with a pencil. My vocal chords are protected but I can still look cool.

The first day often includes some 'getting to know you' games. <u>Refuse to get involved with these.</u> If someone wants to get to know you they can damn well look at your Wikipedia page. If you don't have a Wikipedia page, you should still sit out these silly games (and spend that time setting one up) as it's good to maintain a certain aloofness. Actors who go for the 'no one will ever truly know me' air always get more respect. If the director absolutely insists on you saying something about yourself a good line to go with is 'Hi. My name is (insert name) and the only role I've never been able to play convincingly is me'. Then walk out of the room crying. So many actors forget that they work in the field of 'drama' and should therefore be dramatic at all times.

There is a very real possibility that someone else in the cast will have read this book. I am not a scientist but an artist and therefore can't be bothered to look up the exact figures but I reckon that there's somewhere in the region of 500 million working actors in the world today. If I can get just 10% of those to buy this book then that's probably about 100 million books or something I suppose. Much of the time I had set aside to write this thing has been spent looking up the net worths of JK Rowling and Dan Brown and then planning my future property portfolio accordingly.

So yes, let's assume there's at least one other 'Tips For Actors' disciple in the cast and the stances of 'aloof' and 'dramatic' have been taken. In that instance then go for 'massively enthusiastic actor'. DO get involved in the games. Get involved in them with gusto. When someone else does the standard 'My name is Patrick Stewart. I'm playing Malvolio and I'm a die-hard West Ham fan'-style intro say, 'Wait, Patrick! Wait. Don't stop there. I want to know EVERYTHING about you.' Then when it's your turn – go full pelt. SHARE. And, by all means, get creative…

'Hi, my name is (insert name), I was raised in Derby, close to the mysterious, almost sinister hills of the Peak District and I was breast fed until the age of three. I suppose my first experience of acting was lying to my mother about the women my father brought home while she was toiling away at the mill. I drank my first bottle of hard liquor at the age of nine and it was only when I fell into the loving arms of the 'Cheek by Jowl Theatre Company' at twenty-six that I turned away from the demon drink. I stand before you now, a committed actor, willing to die for each and every one of you and ready to give my all to the cause of playing Portly Villager Number 4.'

That should do it.

AUDITION TIPS

The most important moment in an actor's career is 'the audition'. And I should know – I've had eleven of them! You can spend fourteen years at drama school learning your craft, as I did. You can get up every morning at 5a.m., down a pint of hot water, honey and lemon and plough into your vocal exercises, as I do. You can, like me, spend every Christmas demanding that your family help you prepare for your appearance on *Inside the Actors Studio* with your father role-playing as James Lipton and your mother and siblings as sycophantic students. But if you can't crack 'the audition' then you'll never get anywhere as an actor.

First let's deal with a little myth – the casting couch. For some reason people seem to think that there's a tradition in this industry in which young actresses are invited to sit next to the director on a 'casting couch' and then coerced into giving sexual favours in exchange for work. This may have been true in the past but I can tell you it isn't true now. Most casting departments can't afford a couch. These days the sexual harassment usually takes place on an uncomfortable chair or in a disabled toilet.

TOP TIP!

NEVER go into a casting without a gift for the director. Just rude. Anything under the value of £40 will be seen as insulting

Of course, if you consider yourself a true artist you should never stoop to sacrificing your body and your dignity just to get a role. If on the other hand you have a credit card bill to pay off, here are some tips on sex with a casting director/producer/director...

1. Use the vocal work you did on opening your throat up at drama school when giving a blowjob.

2. Faking orgasms is a great way of showing off your acting but only if you tell them it was fake afterwards.

3. For pillow talk, why not do a speech from your favourite play?

4. Midway through sex go into character as the role you're going for.

5. Say 'I'm just going to slip into something more comfortable'. Then do it massively quickly to show you'll be good at quick changes.

6. Remind them you're good at comedy by doing funny voices throughout the sex.

7. Suggest you do a sexy role play. Then make the role play a scene from the actual show you're auditioning for or maybe just something ludicrously dramatic.

8. Instead of normal sex groans – do vocal exercises to show how professional you are.

9. **Show that you're a professional by insisting on doing a full warm-up before penetration.**

10. **Demonstrate that you're familiar with on-set lingo by saying 'action' when the sex begins and 'cut' when it ends.**

ENTERING THE ROOM

Many actors spend half of their careers just trying to get their foot in the door. What they forget is that the casting director wants to see the rest of their body too. Your objective should be to make an entrance that grabs the attention of everyone in the room.* Most casting decisions are made within five seconds of you walking in. It's almost worth, after five seconds, asking if you've got the part. Don't blow those five seconds with a boring entrance. Grab the room (and each individual in it) by the balls.

Who's in the room? It might just be the casting director, or even an assistant – which is their way of saying they already know they don't want you. There could be a few people there – the director, the writer, some producers. Don't just shake their hands. Be

TOP TIP!
Psyche out the other actors in the casting waiting room by doing an intense physical and vocal warm-up

---

* Make sure, and I can't stress this enough, that you have the right room. I've made many a stunning entrance into a cupboard and then had no entrance energy left for the actual audition.

friendlier than that. Some actors struggle with the quandary of whether to go for the double cheek kiss. I would suggest playing it safe and just kissing them on the lips. Alternatively, you can impress them with just how artistically minded you are by going further than just a double kiss. Go for ten/fifteen kisses. This really says 'I'm well-read, I understand poetry, I've been to India and I got on with the poor people there'.

TOP TIP!
Confidence is everything. Walk into the casting, hand them safety goggles, look them in the eye and say... 'Prepare to be blown away'

TEN GREAT WAYS TO ENTER THE ROOM

1. They're **expecting** you to enter through the door. Surprise them by coming through the window.

2. Show you have an edge by smashing the door open with an axe like Jack Nicholson in *The Shining*.

3. Auditioning to play a cool character? Enter on a motorbike.

4. Show you're a serious method actor by refusing to go in the room until the casting director 'makes me want to'.

5. Going for a younger role? Enter on a skateboard.

6. **Give your entrance atmosphere by adding a smoke machine.**

7. **Smash through some paper like on *Gladiators*.**

8. **Enter to music. I usually go for Fatboy Slim's 'Right Here, Right Now'.**

9. **Auditioning for an action film? Crash through the window on a bungee rope.**

10. **... or crush the director's hand in the hand shake to show how tough you are.**

SMALL TALK

Once you're in there, you're probably not going to be acting immediately. First, they'll test you with some small talk – and it *is* a test. This is your chance to prove that you're interesting. If they ask you how your journey in was, don't bore them with a simple 'Oh, not too bad'. *Entertain* them with an adventurous tale of how you were chased by a pack of wild animals, like in a scene from *Jumanji*. Going for the role of a villain? Tell them you stole a child's ice cream on the way.

Like in every other part of the audition, your primary aim is to be *memorable*. Polite chit chat is not memorable – rudeness is. Tell the casting director you don't like their shirt or a producer that you think she's wearing too much make-up. Say something racist. I actually got thrown out of a casting for doing that a couple of years ago. I'm still waiting to hear back on the job but it was encouraging to know that I had definitely made an impact.

Whatever you do, come prepared with something to talk about. Good topics for small talk include…

- **Electric cigarettes**

- **Your religious beliefs**

- **Rumours you've heard (or made up) about other actors**

- **9/11 conspiracy theories**

- **Hobbies**

- **What's the deal with Ramadan?**

- **Just play the flute for a bit**

- **Show them any medical complaints you have**

- **Whatever happened to Shania Twain?**

- **Flat-pack furniture**

At some stage they will ask you what you've been up to. This isn't a general question. It's a test. They want to know if you've been working. If

TOP TIP!
Impress the casting director by giving them notes on their own performance in reading the other lines

you haven't you need to have a plan to make it sound like you have. If you've recently made a Vine then you're entitled to say 'Oh, I've just finished filming something actually'. If they ask what, just say 'Do you mind if we don't talk about it?' which makes you sound mysterious and cool. Whatever else you've been doing, just try and make it *sound* like you've been acting. If you've been working in a call centre say, 'I've been working a project called "Call Centre"'. If you've been sat at home all day waiting for your agent to ring say, 'I've been working on a project called "Lonely"'.

Eventually, they'll get on to the topic of the script. 'Have you read it?' they'll probably ask. If you have, show them how intelligent you are by giving them a full critique of it. Tell them where you think it goes wrong and what you think could be changed. This will be particularly appreciated by the writer, should they be in the room. Of course, that's not always possible. Some writers are dead – Shakespeare for example. This means that when I'm auditioning for his plays I don't feel the need to be sensitive to the writer's feelings at all and will usually come in with my own rewritten version of the play.

Not having read the script could be frowned upon. In fact, these days actors are often expected to have learnt a couple of scenes for the audition. It's probably something to do with the bloody EU. It's not always possible for you to do that though. You might have got the script at too short notice or perhaps you're a chronic alcoholic. If you don't know it, use it as an opportunity to show how fun you'll be to have around by laughing it off. Take out a bag of cocaine, chop it up on the table and say, 'the only lines I care about are these little beauties!'.

THE ACTING BIT

Sooner or later it will be time to do some actual acting. Some theatre auditions will require you to do a speech. When choosing a monologue, bear in mind that they will see the same speeches again and again. When so many actresses before you have done a Kate from *The Taming of the Shrew*, it's hard to see how you can have your own unique twist on it. That's why you should make every effort to do a speech they haven't seen. How about one from a politician? It is very unlikely that the person before you will have done Nick Clegg's speech to the 2011 Liberal Democrat party conference. It is even more unlikely that

TOP TIP!
Be ruthless. Leave the audition and tell the waiting room that you've been offered the part and have been asked to tell them to go home

they will have seen that speech done in a black, American Deep South voice.

Drama schools usually expect you to prepare one modern and one classical speech. What they're used to seeing is one Shakespeare monologue and something from a contemporary play. Surprise and delight them by reciting a Lil Wayne rap for your modern and a passage from the Bible for your classical.

Television auditions will probably just ask you to read through a couple of scenes with them. Without the set and proper lighting your audition tape isn't going to look as good as you'd like. Give it a professional air by hiring some background artists to walk around behind you.

FINISHING UP

Remember that whilst your audition is going on, there are other actors waiting to be seen after you. They're most probably nervous. Make. Them. Wait. If your audition takes a long time their nerves are likely to get worse and if it really drags on they may even decide to leave. To give your audition maximum length, make as many mistakes as possible. This has the added benefit of giving you extra face time with the decision-makers, which can only be beneficial.

When you do finally leave, show that the time you spent with them really meant something to you by giving everyone a long, meaningful hug.

PLAYING A SMALL PART

'There are no small parts, only small actors'

I certainly subscribe to one half of this famous phrase. There definitely are small actors. Warwick Davis, Judi Dench, Tom Cruise. But are there really no small parts? What if you only have one line? No lines, even. Surely that's a small part? Well, it doesn't have to be. What this phrase teaches us is that it is our duty to ourselves and our careers to make every part we have as big as possible. You may only have one line but the script doesn't tell you how long you should take to say the line. Take the admittedly small line, 'Another drink, sir?'. An unambitious actor might say that line in a second or two. Blink and you might miss it...

I reckon I could make that line last a good five or six minutes. First you could open with a pause. Make that pause as long as you can. Impregnate it with meaning. If you can't think of a specific meaning that works for you then just narrow your eyes and stare meaningfully into the middle distance. That'll do. The audience will assume you're thinking about something deep and give you credit for it. Up until now they have probably been watching a conversation between two leading characters and were engaged in the plot but this is your moment. Consider it your own little one-act play or short film. When, and only when, you feel you have to, start your line but don't rush it...

'A…noth…er…'

Let the audience in on your character's backstory. The other actors have the whole play or film to show off their research. You too have been working for six months on exploring the inner life of your role, 'Bartender', and this is your only chance to show it. For a part like 'Bartender' it is unlikely that you will have had any hints to his back story in the script so it has been your (much harder) job to make it all up. So let's say 'Bartender' grew up in a large working-class family. With so many siblings it was a battle just to be heard so when he speaks he demands attention. His slow, deliberate speech was a very effective technique he developed to make people listen to him…

'A…noth…er'

Being working class it is inevitable that his father was an alcoholic. So the thought of the character in front of him having another drink brings back a litany of torrid memories. It disgusts him…

'D…rink'

There can be an accusatory tone to this word. With so many connotations for him it is unsurprising that the word 'drink' sticks in his throat at first. He can't just blurt it out. And then the final word…

'Sir?'

As we've already established, he's working class which means he's spiritually a communist. The social structures the market-driven economy has created appal him. The very idea that another man could be considered above him, enough so that he should have to call him 'Sir', makes him feel sick. The only way he can say it is if he coats the word in vicious sarcasm…

'Sirrrrrrr?'

Then once the other character replies 'Yes' it's time for your big finale. This is the last time we'll see you so be sure to leave a lasting impression. Don't just hand him the drink. Throw it at him. Then pick up a bottle from the bar, smash it and cut your own face. Now intensely turn the blood into war paint, drawing lines on your cheeks with it, staring directly at the audience or into the camera lens before exiting. I think it's fair to say, you've just stolen the scene…

If a meddling director takes issue with your interpretation of the role of 'Bartender' then just go through your backstory with them. As long as you can prove that you have thought it through and have a reason for each action then there's literally nothing they can do about it…

The point is don't just accept your fate as a bit part. Take the bull by the horns and get people's attention. There is no reason why your cameo can't be the most memorable part of the evening. Here are some ways you can stand out...

1. Wear a fluorescent jacket.

2. Keep the audience's attention on you by spinning round three times after each of your lines.

3. Persistently fall over during the other actors' dialogue.

4. Or hum while they're speaking.

5. Playing a servant with no lines? Make sure they do by giving your character Tourette's.

6. Undermine the lead actor by standing behind them in their big emotional moment and rolling your eyes.

7. Get a friend to sit in the audience and shine a laser pen on your forehead.

8. Inhale helium before each of your lines.

9. Give your character the hiccups.

10. Get noticed by being the only actor who's mysteriously not standing in the light.

CRYING

The greatest indicator of an actor's skill is their ability to cry on command. The very best actors can cry roughly five pints of tears a day. In her early days Meryl Streep would sit at home every day weeping gallons of tears like some kind of tear factory. She would then turn up at auditions with large vats of the stuff. The people in charge immediately knew that there was no need for her to read the script for them. Anyone who could produce that kind of volume of tears was clearly a fine actress and could turn her hand to any role. History tells us that they, and the giant tanks of Streep tears, were right.[*]

If you are able to cry on command, then you should be looking to show off that skill at every opportunity. In the audition, in your head shot, throughout every performance. There really is no limit. If you're ever at an industry party and talking to a director don't bore them with small talk. That doesn't show them that you can act. Crying does! Actresses have an unfair reputation for being emotionally fragile or somehow 'crazy'. They're not. They are just showing the world what they can do.

Not everyone finds crying so easy. Some actors, no matter how hard they try, can never seem to get themselves to the place in which they can turn the water works on. There is an industry term for these people and that is: 'dead inside'.

[*]   And what became of those tears? Amy Adams recently bought them at auction and filled her swimming pool with what she refers to as 'acting juice'.

If you suffer from internal deadness then all is not lost. There are ways in which you can force yourself to cry.

The most common way is to think of something that upsets you. It might be a hurtful thing someone has said to you or the thought of losing a loved one. For me it is the success of people I went to drama school with. If I ever need to cry for a role I start by looking at the IMDb pages of some of the more successful actors from my class, counting their credits and comparing them to mine. One particular former classmate has gone on to become quite famous so I then go on to search them on YouTube and look for especially sycophantic interviews. The thought that it could have been me on *Loose Women* and not them is so painful to me that I am crying now as I write this. Who turned up for class three hours early every single day of drama school? Me. Not them. Who showed their commitment by wearing a different tight-fitting black vest every day? Me. Not them. Who chose not to talk to the visiting agents after the showcase, but be a fucking professional and do a 45-minute warm-down? Me. Not them. And yet who has just signed another twelve-month contract with *Emmerdale*? Them. Not me. I feel sick.

TOP TIP!
Real actors cry. In every production, no matter how small their part, each actor should cry at least once

If you've been fortunate enough to avoid the kind of emotional misery I have been plagued by you may have to use more artificial tricks. One technique is to disguise sweat as tears. Simply apply roll-on anti-perspirant to your entire face, only missing out where tear tracks would form. Then do some vigorous cardio and await your scene-stealing moment.

We all know that chopping onions makes us cry. This is a great one to use in close-ups. Thirty per cent of the onions bought in LA go on to be chopped just out of shot by actors.

With the amount of money that is spent on big Hollywood movies these days, many directors don't like taking the risk of being at the mercy of an actor's crying or chopping skills. That's why many of them have taken the on-set crying into their own hands. Remote-controlled artificial tear ducts are the future and are being used on more and more movie sets every year. All the director needs to do is press a button and they're in business – actor tears! The only downside is that it is enormously painful for the actor and does in about a third of cases lead to permanent blindness. But surely that's a small price to pay for a good scene?

> ## INTERESTING FACT!
> In acting there are NO performance-enhancing drugs. Except for cocaine.

COMEDY

It's good to laugh and for me personally, one of the things I find funniest is (I hope I'm not alone in this) comedy. And who is it who makes comedy funny? Actors. There are countless comedy actors who make me howl with laughter – the guy who played Joey in *Friends*, the woman who played Rachel in *Friends*, the guy who played Chandler in *Friends*, the woman who played Phoebe in *Friends* – the list is endless. Without actors comedy would just be words on a page. There is no way that anyone could ever just laugh at words on a page. No one ever laughed at a book!

Comedic acting isn't easy, it takes practice. But you won't get comic roles unless you can do comic acting. It's a catch-22. How can you get the practice if you can't get the roles? You're going to have to find somewhere else to hone your comedic skills. Start trying to make your dramatic roles funny. Playing a mother who's just been told that her son has been in a car crash? See if you can get a laugh by crying in a funny voice. Playing a man who's just been convicted of a crime he did not

TOP TIP!
If you don't feel in character 10 mins before the performance ask the stage manager to cancel the show. The audience will understand

commit? Try out a prat fall as your character enters the courtroom.

Now you've got the practice, you're starting to get cast in comic roles but it isn't necessarily plain sailing from here on in. You will find there's moments when you're struggling to get laughs in places that you feel you should do. Here, you have to remember that old adage – comedy is all about timing. A simple pause can make all the difference. It is a scientific fact that the longer the pause between a set-up and a punchline – the bigger the laugh will be. Be brave! If it takes a 45-minute pause to get the chuckle you're after then so be it.

If you're still not getting the laughs you're after, there are a number of tricks you can try...

- **Physically tickle the audience.**

- **Laugh after every joke, so the audience know what they're supposed to do.**

- **If a joke doesn't get a laugh, it might be that they don't understand it. Turn and explain it to the audience. 'You see, that was funny because…'**

- **If in doubt, fall over.**

- **Ask a technician to throw in lots of funny sound effects.**

- **Do a fart.**

- Maybe there's something wrong with the script. Just tell a joke you saw on something else.

- Wear a novelty T-shirt that says something hilarious like 'My idea of a balanced diet is a beer in each hand'. I'm laughing just typing it.

- Or pull out a funny novelty dildo.

If all else fails just pretend that the show isn't actually funny and is supposed to be a very serious piece.

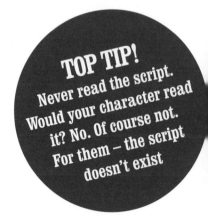

TOP TIP!
Never read the script. Would your character read it? No. Of course not. For them – the script doesn't exist

LEARNING LINES

After 'Have you had any work since you last signed on?' the second most asked question of actors is 'How do you learn your lines?'. The answer is 'With difficulty'.

It is a medical fact that over the course of an actor's career their brain will enlarge by roughly 150% as a direct result of all the lines they learn. That doesn't mean it's not still difficult to fit it all in. If you have a big part to learn, the only way to do it is to give your brain a good clear out. Get rid of any information you don't need. Start with the obvious stuff – phone numbers, friends' birthdays, whatever's going on in the news.

That may not be enough though. The part of Hamlet is absolutely enormous. Most actors who play that role end up shedding every bit of memory they have that isn't directly connected to the piece – their partner's faces, how to feed and bathe themselves. Spending time with an actor who's playing Hamlet whilst they're off stage is literally like being in the company of someone with severe dementia. But it's an absolutely essential part of learning the lines. Great performances come at a price.

Making space is one thing, but what techniques can we use to insert the lines into the brain? Amongst other things I subscribe to the unproven method of printing the script out, eating it, swallowing it and then allowing the body to ingest the information. Does it work? I don't know. Has it ruined many a vegetable soup? Yes. Have my insides been irreparably damaged by the ink? Hard to say. Will I continue to do it? Until someone can prove to me categorically that it doesn't work – absolutely.

You can of course learn them by asking someone to test you on your lines. Be careful with this. Working with someone without high-level acting training isn't advisable – bad habits are contagious. Sometimes you don't have any other options though. Once I found myself running through some lines with somebody who trained at some ghastly northern drama school. All seemed fine at first. The lines went into my head and I was able to do the scene perfectly well. But three months later I sprained my ankle. Coincidence? I don't think so.

When you're running through lines it's good to be doing an action as you do it. This means that when you say them they won't sound like they're read from a script – they'll sound like a living, breathing thing. My favourite time to run lines is during sex. Advantages include…

1. **It engages my partner in what I'm working on at the time.**

2. **It helps me to withhold orgasm.**

3. **If I'm working on Shakespeare, the iambic pentameter gives the sex a nice kind of rhythm.**

4. **It can give the scene a new angle I wouldn't have otherwise thought of.**

5. **In case I forget the lines while we're doing it, I can place the script on my partner's back.**

They say that a dog is a man's best friend. Well, if that man (or woman) is an actor man (or woman) then I would have to disagree – it's their agent. A good agent is someone who is there for their clients whenever they need them. If you're banged up in a Cambodian prison with one phone call – you call your agent. If you hit a deer on a country road and are not sure what to do – you call your agent. If you're on a Welsh campsite at two in the morning and after walking through 150 feet of mud discover that the toilets don't have toilet paper, assuming you brought your phone with you to use as a torch – you call your agent.[*]

Some would find this level of dependency excessive but it's not as if agents are expected to do all of this out of the kindness of their hearts. We give them 10-15% of our incomes. That can be as much as £400 a year! That's a lot more than AA breakdown cover and yet some agents still refuse to come out and fix their clients' gearboxes when they need them the most. Not on.

TOP TIP!
Ask your agent to come to your audition and sit beside you saying things like 'oh, that's very good' while you're acting

---

[*]   I have done that last one on no less than seven occasions.

If you are lucky enough to find a good agent – do everything you can to maintain a good relationship. Agents are human beings (except in Japan where they're all robots) so it is only natural that they favour the clients they get on with best. This is a tough industry. You are constantly in competition with other actors – most of all, the rest of your agent's client list. Your aim should be to *always* be at the front of their mind so that you're the first person they think to put up for jobs.

Start every day by texting your agent. Nothing creepy. Just a simple 'Hello you. x'. Then at about 9.30 a.m. give them a call at the office to ask how their journey in was. It's their job to care about you but rarely does a client care about *them*. Showing them that you do can only help your cause.

Give them another call at about 11 a.m. to ask about something specific. Follow up on an audition you've had or maybe suggest that they put you up for a project you've heard about. I usually just go to Russell Crowe's IMDb page and see what's in pre-production.

> 'I hear there's going to be a Les Misérables 2. I'd like to be seen for it.'

Phone calls aren't enough to stay in their heads though. Your mission now is to find an excuse to go in to the office. One of my favourite techniques is to pretend that I'm going to be running the London Marathon for charity and am looking for sponsors.

'What a good guy he is,' I can almost hear the assistants say. 'How does he find the time?'

Now that you're in the office, find a way to stay as long as you can. Maybe it's raining, maybe you fake an asthma attack – whatever works. One trick I'm fond of is asking if I can use one of the office computers to send an email. I then use that opportunity to ruin as many of their clients' CVs as I possibly can. The intention being that I become their only bookable actor.

I am not currently represented by anyone. I'm not exactly sure why. It always seems like things are going great but then they send me an email saying the agency is going in a new direction that doesn't include me. I guess I just haven't found the right one for me. The closest I came was when I accepted a stalker's offer of representation. Ruth's contacts within the industry weren't strong but her attention to detail was fantastic. I really felt like she was there for me whenever I needed her and she even offered to move in with me so that we could work on my career 24/7. Unfortunately, just as she was about to, *Two Pints of Lager* really took off and she moved her attentions onto Ralf Little.

DRAMA SCHOOL TIPS

In history, four actors have achieved professional status without attending drama school. All of them were dead before their time.

The first was a silent movie star named Wilfie Butterbean. Wilfie had a talent for pulling faces that landed him leading roles in turgid comedies such as *Butterbean Express* and *Wilfie and the Wog*. Without the emotional underpinning that drama school could have given his face pulling, the public's love affair with Butterbean was short-lived. After making 22 films over a fortnight in 1923, the work dried up and he was reduced to performing at end-of-pier variety shows. The schedule was demanding, with upwards of eight shows a day. Having never been taught to properly warm up, Wilfie's face couldn't take the strain. In the summer of 1924, at the age of 21, Wilfie Butterbean died of face cancer. He left behind a wife and nine children.

It's a cautionary tale for anyone thinking of making the step into professional acting without serious training. DRAMA SCHOOL IS ESSENTIAL. But how should one behave on their first day of training?

The first day of anything will always give the nerves a good wracking. Drama school is no different. You will be making judgements about your new peers, so you are of course aware, that they will be judging you. It is important to let them know just how serious you are about acting.

Dress actor! Men: stubble, leather jacket, shirt with at least six buttons undone and an indoor scarf. Women: black leggings, bare feet, cheap tank top, bottle of Evian and an indoor scarf.

Early on you will most likely each be asked to introduce yourselves and say something about you. This is your chance to let everyone know the kind of actor you are. Here's a suggestion...

'Hi, my name's Mark and I was born a crack baby.'

This will send you straight to the top of the class. It says, I'm interesting, I have a lot of experience to draw on, I will be difficult to work with, I am amazing.

Note – don't worry about whether it's true or not. The important thing is that they believe you. Both you and I know that the likelihood of an actual crack baby getting close to drama school is next to zero.

'Hi, my name's Sarah aaaaaaand…' – then break into a song from your favourite musical.

This tells us that you are a musical actor and are not prepared to do any dialogue sans melody. This is a reasonable request but it's vital you set your stall out early on. I know many an actor, who could have been in the chorus of a touring production of *Wicked*, who've found themselves stuck in some godforsaken HBO drama. Perhaps if they had set their boundaries from the off then they could have avoided such a miserable fate.

'Privy. My given name is Stephen and fortune hath brought me to this place weary but full of merriment and mirth.'

What's that across the room? It's a teacher writing a tick next to your name. Those who can handle the Bard will always gain the most respect. Just learn the sentence I have given you. Worry about who 'the Bard' is later on.

Now that everyone knows what you're about it's time to start acting, right? Wrong. The rest of the day, and most likely the next two years, will be spent playing warm-up games and working on your voice and posture.

This is entirely appropriate. You're not ready. In the Sixties a working-class drama school was set up in which the students started acting from day one. Big mistake. There were so many instances of people dropping props on their toes and falling off the stage that they spent more time in A&E than anywhere else. BE PATIENT. It's a marathon, not a sprint.[*]

TOP TIP!
If you find yourself working with someone who didn't go to drama school ask to have them removed from the cast. Seems harsh but safety first

---

[*] Women should be aware that unless they have secured a major role by the time they are 24 their career is, to all intents and purposes, over.

You are likely to encounter three different types of teacher at drama school…

THE TRADITIONALIST

This old public school gent has been teaching at the school since 1974. He will work with you on the more technical things like Shakespeare, text work and how to maintain a pretentious reverence to the theatre at all times. He does not own a television or a mobile phone and drinks exactly one glass of red wine every lunch time.

THE RENEGADE

A different type of man altogether. Bitter at his own lack of success, as an actor he is prone to moments of almost violent rage. He takes great joy in telling each of the students why they will never make it. Ever the experimentalist, nearly every one of his exercises involves the more attractive girls in the class getting naked. He will often be found in the pub having drinks bought for him by impressionable first years.

MOTHER EARTH

Usually a voice teacher, this profoundly spiritual woman will act as a sort of therapist to the students. Most of her classes involve a lot of 're-experiencing the womb' work. As the school's chief Alexander Technique expert she spends a great deal of time touching up her pupils. Passionate about posture, she regularly weeps at the sight of slumped shoulders.

OPINION!
If you enjoy acting then you're doing it wrong. Acting is about experiencing intense emotional pain in different accents.

ANIMAL WORK

A common workshop at drama school is 'animal work' in which students study and then pretend to be animals. This is strange to civilians. What possible benefit can be drawn from spending hours as a chicken? The answer is simple… 'Loads of benefit'.

For a start, many actors get their first break playing animals. Russell Crowe started out playing Bouncer in the Australian soap opera *Neighbours* and who could forget Christian Bale's first big screen role beside Tom Hanks in *Turner and Hooch*? Already committed to method acting, Bale spent two years working as a police dog in preparation. Of course you wouldn't recognise Bale in the film. He was one of the first actors to learn to shape-shift into other creatures and objects. To this day, when between jobs Bale will often keep his acting muscle fit by using his shape-shifting skills to play a chair in the Queen Vic on *EastEnders* or Ashton Kutcher's trousers on *Two and a Half Men*.

But let's get back to animal work. Before you've done it it can seem quite an embarrassing prospect. Unless you've already done some porn work the chances are you haven't spent a great deal of time crawling around on your hands and knees. At first your head will be filled with doubts. 'How is this helping me to be a better actor?', 'I can't believe I'm going into thousands of pounds of crippling debt for this', 'Why am I curiously aroused?'.

Like with almost anything at drama school the key is to trust. Trust that the teachers know what they're doing. If they didn't then how would they have got jobs teaching acting? They wouldn't. They'd be stuck in some dead-end professional acting job. No. Teachers are the crème de la crème. That's why they can earn as much as £11,000 a year.

Once you've accepted the idea of pretending to be an animal, you have to choose which creature you're going to be. Here are some suggestions...

PARROT This is the only animal which allows you to give yourself lines. Use it to undermine your classmates with phrases like 'You've put on weight. You've put on weight'.

CAT Cats nap a lot so this is a great choice for when you're hungover. Curl up into a ball in the corner of the room, sleep off last night's booze and get extra points for 'staying in character'.

DOG Use this animal as a subtle way of letting fellow classmates or the teacher know you like them by humping their leg.

TORTOISE Tortoises are slow. If at any point in the rest of the term you are slow in remembering your lines you can use this as an excuse, 'I'm sorry. The tortoise is still with me'.

WILD BEAR This gives you a great opportunity to violently maul an annoying classmate whilst at the same time getting praise for being convincing.

OPINION!
The fewer people who come and see your play the more arty and therefore better it is

SHOWCASE TIPS

At the end of your drama school journey[*] comes the showcase. Here you will perform a speech with the hope of getting an agent and possibly even some interest from casting directors. If you mess it up your life is essentially over. I'm serious. Some of the people I went to drama school with failed to get representation and now they are just teachers, lawyers, small business owners, loving parents – nobodies.

The only way to avoid that fate is to put every ounce of effort you can into your monologue. Think carefully about what speech you choose. Agents want to feel that you're a sellable commodity, someone who'll actually get work. You need to show that you can offer something that others in the marketplace can't.

Let's say that you're a white man. So what? There are only so many white male roles. What separates you? Why not do a speech blacked-up? Show that you can play across the races. Remember, this is your big chance! Don't let the opportunity pass you by by playing a character you are actually likely to be cast as. That's what everyone else will be doing!

That brings us on to your classmates. There is no getting away from the fact that you are now in direct competition with the people you have shared the last three years with.

---

[*]   Always refer to your time at drama school as a 'journey'. It just sounds good.

Any laughs or moments of kindness you have shared are now over. They're dead. Now it's down to the cut-throat world of semi-professional acting. Kill or be killed.

Use your speech as an opportunity to not only display your own skills but also to denigrate your competition. How? Write your own monologue and in it play a 'character' who reveals unhelpful facts about each of the other students…

'You know, it's been a crazy three years at this here drama school…'

In this example I am imagining you using a sort of Wild West accent. As I said, you still have to show off your abilities.

'I remember way back when we all started out – Pippa Harvey had herself a dog gone lisp and she still ain't got rid of that little sucker. Boy, have we had some wild old times?! Hey guys! Y'all remember when little Robert Harrison forgot his lines in that Brecht production we did? And what about when Sam Flanagan said that he didn't like Shakespeare? Crazy days.'

Just go methodically through your whole class and watch with glee as the agents cross them off their lists. Don't worry, you'll still be able to laugh about it in the bar afterwards. (Show)business is (show)business. They'll understand.

WHAT OCCUPIES AN ACTOR'S MIND AT ANY ONE TIME…

0.20% How their family are.

0.80% The job they're doing.

19% Whether they look fat in their head shot.

80% The rights and wrongs of sleeping with extras/ushers.

TELEVISION ACTING

An actor's life is a constant battle between doing things of artistic merit (Shakespeare, mask work, stilt walking) and things devoid of any artistic worth (film, television, commercial theatre) to pay the bills. Personally, I have avoided such a conflict by keeping my expenditure down to such a low level that I can survive solely on a few weeks Theatre-in-Education work a year. See the 'Living Frugal' chapter for more info(rmation).

But if you are one of those actors who has succumbed to the comforts of central heating and regular public transport use then you will need to, on occasion, prostitute yourself to the world of television. And I don't use the word prostitute without thought. Metaphorically you will be stripping yourself bare and allowing the philistine televisual sphere* to penetrate you in exchange for a daily rate plus repeat fees. Metaphorically.

Your first task is to get the job. To do that you need to earn the respect of those in charge at your audition.

---

*   It is phrases like 'philistine televisual sphere' which set this book out from the rest of the acting advice literature market. I would go so far as to say that that phrase is actually too good for this niche field. If anyone from a larger, less tin pot publisher is interested in signing me up for a novel I'm willing to talk. That is just a taster of what I am capable of. In fact 'Philistine Televisual Sphere' is a great title. We can discuss what the book would actually be about at a later date. I'm thinking maybe a seedy TV executive murders a series of underlings using a deadly spiked sphere he carries around with him. As I say, I am writing this book right now and have literally just had this idea so it's not fully formed but if you (Penguin, HarperCollins, Faber & Faber) want to send me a serious figure I will take a serious look at it.

The people who make TV know that what they make is rubbish. Show that you understand that by saying as you walk in…

'Ok. So what crap are we churning out for the masses today?'

Instantly, they will recognise that you get what television is all about. Convince them further still by showing them that, unlike perhaps some of the other candidates, you've also watched television. Do this by rapping the theme tune to *The Fresh Prince of Bel Air*. This is, so I am told, how James Gandolfini got the role of Tony Soprano.

The chances are they will offer you the job there and then. If they don't, please refer to my 'sex with casting directors' section. Don't be afraid to take this book out during the audition. It shows initiative.

So, you've got the job. Let me guide you through the day. Most television acting involves getting up very early. The bad news is that this means you may have to restrict yourself to just half a bottle of Tia Maria the night before. The good news is that they will usually provide you with a driver to take you to set.

When getting into the car it is important to set out some ground rules. If the driver wants to chat and you don't, immediately ask if you can have the radio on. If you're feeling charitable, suggest Magic FM as this is the favourite radio station of ALL taxi drivers. The relentlessly cheery music helps them to forget about the mistakes they made in their lives that led them to becoming a taxi driver. If you can't quite stand the thought of Phil Collins in the morning then hand them a CD of your radio work, ask them to put it on and pretend to fall asleep.

Alternatively, you may want to get your vocal chords moving and decide to actually engage in a conversation. Be aware that the driver is likely to find your perfect drama school pronunciation intimidating. Make him feel more comfortable by dropping a few 'hs' and 'ts' and throwing in the odd 'cor blimey, take a look at that tasty bit of jogging crumpet'. Try to stay on topics he feels happy talking about. For a taxi driver these include immigration and… actually it's just immigration.

You may want to use your time in the taxi to prepare for your day's work. It is, for example, a great chance to learn your lines. Why not get the driver to help you out? Hand him a script, ask him to give it everything and go for it! The great thing is that at 5 a.m. there aren't really any other cars on the road so safety isn't a problem.

Your journey in can be a moment to reflect upon how far you've come in your career. A few years ago I'm proud to say I was cast in an advert for Crunchy Nut Cornflakes. As we made our way to the set I was finding it hard to comprehend just what I had achieved by getting such a job. I asked the driver to make a detour to where it all began for me – my primary school. We parked outside for a while and I thought about how that little boy who all those years ago, absolutely nailed the role of second shepherd couldn't have dreamt of such heights. I wiped away my tears, collected my thoughts and we made our way to the set. Unfortunately, thanks to a dodgy sat nav and Dorset being a lot further away from West London than I had remembered we were actually far too late and by the time we got there I had been replaced. Still, no regrets.

If you're filming 'on location' you will first be taken to what is known as 'unit base'. This is usually in an industrial car park in the middle of nowhere. The reason for this, I suspect, is so that if an extra dies in an on-set accident, it's an easy place to make a body 'disappear'.

Upon leaving the car you will be greeted by the second AD or if the production company doesn't think you're actually that talented, a runner. They will take you to your trailer. The size and quality of your trailer is a good indication of how valued you are as an actor. I like to make a point of beginning trailer negotiations before the audition. Yes, I rarely work. But at least I can be confident that when I do, I will have somewhere appropriate to relax in-between scenes.

The top Hollywood A-Listers' trailers are truly a sight to behold. The stuff of *MTV Cribs*. Eight storeys high, with their own indoor swimming pool, games room and state of the art discotheques. What Judi Dench asks for – she gets. Fair enough. But you may find your trailer is not quite the same. On my very first TV job I had to share my trailer with a large Somalian family who were waiting to be processed for asylum. We're still in touch as it happens.

Once you've had some time to settle in your trailer, you will be invited to go to the catering truck and get some breakfast. Over the years fees for actors in television have remained stagnant whilst the cost of living continues to rise. The catering truck is one of the few places where an actor can claim what they truly deserve. On any television job, your aim should be to eat as much as possible. For breakfast – order everything. Twice. If you can't stomach a dozen hash browns in one sitting, stick some in your bag and take them home to your family. At lunch there are usually three or four meal options from the catering truck and a table with a selection of cold salads and meats. Eat as much as you are physically able to. Then go back for dessert. AS IS YOUR RIGHT!

There is the danger that the amount of food your body will be digesting will affect your performance. Ask someone to hold a

TOP TIP!
Never talk to the crew. These are the same people who bullied you at school. They are not your friends

sick bucket just out of shot. THAT'S WHAT RUNNERS ARE FOR. Then incorporate anything your body might me doing into your performance. Is your face going red and sweaty? Good. Use it! Your *character's* face is now going red and sweaty because they are feeling nervous, stressed, angry, in love – whatever is going on in the scene.

Television acting offers us an opportunity we are not afforded in the world of theatre… the chance to make mistakes. If you mess up a line in a play – that's it. The moment's gone, you've probably ruined the play and there's a good chance that the bulk of the audience will be heading for the exits. In television you can always simply do another take. Don't be afraid to take advantage of that. Use up as many takes as you need. The director won't mind. Some actors don't really start to get into the swing of things until the 60th or 70th take. And that's ok. It's not like a TV set is under time constraints. A theatre has to close by a certain time. With TV, you can always just come back the next day to get it right.

CLOSE-UPS

As any actor knows, the most important shot is the close-up. Here, every tiny blemish, every flicker of the eyes can be seen in minute detail. It is said that the Ancient Egyptians believed that an HD TV camera could see into your very soul. When the camera is tight onto your face, it's very easy to look like you're overacting. So remember this… LESS IS MORE.

It seems crazy but the LESS you do, the BETTER you will look at acting. Therefore, it stands to reason that if you do ABSOLUTELY NOTHING you will look BRILLIANT at acting. So don't react to anything. Don't say your lines. Don't even learn them. Just take a valium and sit there, completely still, exuding award-worthy excellence.

THE CREW

There are so many people working on a set, it's hard to work out what everyone does. Here's a guide.

FOCUS PULLER

This person is on set at all times with the sole purpose of keeping the actors on their toes. They will literally 'pull focus' from the actors by doing things like juggling and eating fire. The actors' egos are then wounded by the attention not being on them, so they up their performances to get it back.

BEST BOY

This comes from an old Hollywood tradition. When a film crew arrived in a new place, the village elders would present their finest youngster or 'best boy' to the director for sacrifice. The tradition stands today, although the 'Best Boy' is usually just asked to make tea rather than ritually burnt for the amusement of studio executives.

MAKE-UP ARTIST

The make-up department have to be at the unit base before anyone else. Day in, day out, they are there setting up their make-up truck, as early as 4 a.m. and yet they are usually the cheeriest people on set. That is because they get to spend one on one time with the greatest people on earth – actors.

One of the functions of a make-up artist is obvious – to apply make-up. The other is less apparent but just as important – to laugh at the jokes of male actors. The success or failure of every production depends almost entirely on the level each actor's ego is at. The focus puller reigns that ego in. The make-up artist builds it up.

TOP TIP!
Be careful where you get your acting tips from. There's a lot of bad advice out there

DIRECTOR

The director is in charge of everything – a kind of puppeteer. In fact, in a lot of low-budget soap operas in which they can't afford proper actors – the director will actually operate the cast with invisible strings.

WARDROBE ASSISTANT

Be warned. All wardrobe assistants are perverts who have specifically chosen to do the job in which they are most likely to see actors in their underwear. There are hundreds of different jobs in the entertainment industry. Only one requires you to stand next to an actor whilst they dress and undress, trying on a series of outfits until you tell them that they can stop.

They are though, natural geeks, not cool enough to be actors and are therefore more afraid of you than you are of them. If you omit to wear any underwear at all, then when stripping shout 'Is this what you want to see? Well? Is it?' That usually wards them off a bit.

TOP TIP!
Help the director out by saying 'action' and 'cut' yourself

And they are 'extras'. I will not accept this new fashionable phrase – supporting artists. They are not artists. Rembrandt is an artist. Mozart is an artist. Adam Woodyatt is an artist. The average extra brings no more to a production than the chairs they are so fond of sitting on.

That being said, in some very rare cases, extras have been known to turn their work into an art form. Robert De Niro was one. In the late 60s and early 70s he appeared in the background of a number of movies. He was so good that the audience would be watching Julie Andrews or Robert Redford or whoever else was in the foreground and then suddenly they'd be saying to themselves 'Wait! What was that fantastic blur that just went past?'. That blur would be Robert De Niro. But he wouldn't be a blur for much longer. That was because he had what it took to be a real actor. Most extras do not.

They think they do though. Look out for them. If for some reason you feel that a scene isn't working – but you can't put your finger on why – an extra is most likely at fault. Somewhere in the back of *your* shot, there they are, sat at a table, talking quietly to yet another extra *ruining* your scene. Even if there is no truth to it, they really do make great scapegoats. If you're stumbling over your lines, just blame it on the extras being distracting. 'Can you ask the extras to keep the background chat down please?'. Even if they're not making any noise at all, no one will question you. That is because on a set, extras are the lowest of the low. Use that to your advantage. Late to the set? Blame it on an extra. Some money has gone missing from the petty cash? Blame it on an extra. Failed to lose the ten pounds you said that you would for the role? Blame it on an extra.

NEVER, under any circumstances, talk to an extra. They are essentially legalised stalkers and you will only encourage them. That is unless you are single and quite fancy them. In which case, feel free to use your status as someone with lines to get yourself laid.

INTERESTING FACT!
You are never more than 10 feet away from an out of work actor

RADIO ACTING TIPS

Imagine if you were doing a performance to a packed theatre of silent blind people with your feet strapped to the ground. That is what acting for the radio is like. Many actors never get to experience it but if you can I highly recommend it. For a start, you can earn in excess of £35 a day – not to be sniffed at!

In Britain the vast majority of radio acting occurs on BBC Radio 4. You are therefore legally required to be at least 75% middle class by birth to do it. I've seen many a hopeful cockney oik turned away from the Maida Vale studios, trudging back to his soot-covered family with his cap in hand. It's hard not to feel sorry for them, but until Talk Sport starts producing radio plays that's the way it's going to be.

There are many advantages to acting on the radio. The first is that you don't have to learn the lines. Thanks to the fact that you can't be seen, you can literally stand there and read them from the script. I see this as cheating though. I consider myself to have failed as an actor if I have to refer to a script so I will always do my best to learn it. Often the producer will complain that I've been holding up proceedings for three hours and it really would be easier for everyone involved if I could just 'pick up the fucking script and say the fucking words'. I am a proud professional though and refuse to do it. Sure, I end up paraphrasing the lines a little but I think the audience can tell the difference between an actor reading from a script and a true actor who (pretty much) knows his lines.

Actors who do insist on reading from the script suffer from the problem of paper noise. The rustle of a script page being turned can jolt the audience out of wherever they imagine the action to be taking place. Luckily most Radio 4 actors have a private income so they hire children from the Third World as page turners. The children are whipped if they make a noise but are so skillful that this rarely happens. I have heard liberal do-gooders moan about the persistent paper cuts on the children's hands but, I have to say, you can't get a show as good as *The Archers* without some sacrifice.

Being not seen does mean that the costume budget is next to nothing and many actors end up paying for their own. A few years ago I had two words as a police officer in a Radio 4 drama set in the 1920s. Getting the exact uniform an officer from my particular force would have worn cost me two weeks and £1200 and I will admit to being disappointed when the line 'Yes, Sergeant' was cut from the final edit. I think it was worth it though, just to get the authenticity.

Despite my attention to detail when it comes to costume, radio is undeniably an audio medium. This means that clarity of voice is absolutely essential. The only way to ensure that you have this is to be constantly drinking liquids. Before each line, the average radio actor will drink two pints of hot water, honey and lemon and a large bottle of Evian. This doesn't come without one obvious drawback – full bladders. So when a radio actor walks into a studio they are fitted with a catheter. This is a sensible precaution and aids the smooth running of the recording.

The only incident I heard of it going wrong was at a radio recording session in Los Angeles. It was a large production with about 25 people in the room. They'd been going for about 5 hours and were nearly ready for a bag change when disaster struck – earthquake tremor. No one was hurt but the studio did suddenly find itself two feet deep in actors' urine.

INTERESTING FACT!
A matinee is about half the length of the evening show and is usually performed by the cast's children/pets

VOICEOVER TIPS

If you're lucky you might one day get to try your hand at voiceover acting. This can be rather lucrative particularly for the man who does the voice of Siri. It does though, take up literally all of his time. There are so many variants on what Siri might be asked that it would be impossible to pre-record everything. And you never know when someone might have a question for Siri so it means being on call 24/7. Right now, at this very moment, he is locked in a studio in San Francisco firing out answers to people from all around the world.

The chances are you won't get the Siri job though. You could find yourself doing something far more low-key like voicing a detergent commercial or a weaponised robot employed by an authoritarian state to police its people.

TOP TIP!
NEVER EVER do an advert unless you truly believe in the product or the money is quite good

Either way, it pays well, so you'll want to create a good impression in your first voiceover session. Upon entering the key is to look like you're really experienced and know what you're doing. As you go into the booth you'll be handed some headphones and placed in front of what is known as a 'microphone'. Look at the microphone and see if it has a maker's name on it. If it does, say something like the following...

'Ah, Bosch. Lovely bit of kit that is.'

The engineer and producer will immediately be impressed that they are dealing with a pro.

When considering what accent or voice to do, you need to think about what you're talking about...

Advert which mentions football – Northern, preferably Geordie.

Gambling advert aimed at men – Cockney wide-boy.

Gambling advert aimed at women – Bubbly Welsh woman.

Pensions advert – R.P.

Bank advert – Really nice humble guy with indiscernible accent.

Irish tourism advert – Irish.

Australian tourism advert – Australian.

American tourism advert – Really nice humble guy with indiscernible accent.

Movie trailer – Movie trailer voice.

TOP TIP!
Sometimes it can feel like you'll never make it. Don't give up. In six month you could be voicing a murdered stripper on Grand Theft Auto

OUT OF WORK ACTOR'S
DAILY ROUTINE

5 a.m. Rise.

5.02 a.m. Bikram yoga session. Helps you stay on the ball.

7 a.m. Go to a location shoot and get free breakfast from the catering van. Eggs should be poached, not fried. You're not an animal.

7.05 a.m. Try and 'bump' into the producer on the catering bus. Be as vague as possible about why you're there despite having nothing to do with the production. 'Just passing by. Thought I'd see what you guys are up to.' Don't worry if you've never met them. They'll just assume they've forgotten you.

8 a.m. Go to a park with a friend and perform a duologue for any passersby. This allows you to say at your next audition that you've 'been busy'.

10 a.m. Practise characterisation. Find an odd-looking person and follow them, aping their movements. I once found myself doing this with the then Home Secretary Charles Clarke. Knowing nothing of politics (for me, theatre is the only news

I need) I assumed he was one of those tramps who wear suits. It was only when I found myself in an office and recognised John Prescott from *Celebrity Mr and Mrs* that I realised I was in fact in Cabinet.

Midday. Pop into your agent's office because you were 'in the neighbourhood'. Bring a gift. Fudge or grapes or something. Your agent will say things are really quiet at the moment. Make a joke about their most successful client e.g. 'Quiet for Bennedict is it?'. Do a big laugh to show you're joking, followed by an intense stare to show you're actually quite serious. Kiss everyone twice on the cheek (except the accounts department) and leave.

---

1 p.m. Go for lunch with an actor friend. Talk about how things are really quiet lately but you've 'been really lucky actually'. If you've done a day's work, on *Doctors* for example, within the last eighteen months, then you're entitled to say 'I've just finished shooting something'. The aim is for them to come away from the conversation feeling that their career is going awfully compared to yours.

---

2 p.m. Go to a theatre holding a matinee and ask if the whole cast have turned up yet. Explain that if they haven't, you're willing to step in. They will have. Go home.

3 p.m. Watch six hours of *Actors Studio* videos on YouTube.

9 p.m. Go on your Spotlight profile and check that there's nothing you can add. School plays perhaps?

10 p.m. Head back into town and get into the Phoenix by saying you're in *Jersey Boys*. Drink water all night but pretend you're drunk. Use your fake inebriation as an excuse to loudly sing songs from musicals, display dance moves and perform monologues. This is your best chance of 'being seen' at the moment.

2 a.m. Arrive home. Google everyone you've met tonight and directly compare their careers with yours. Assess their number of IMDb credits versus age ratios. If you come out well, treat yourself to another *Actors Studio* video.

3/4 a.m. Sleep.

5 a.m. Repeat.

INTERESTING FACT!
If you cut a true actor open – they BLEED theatre… you know, props and lights and stuff

GAMES

THE PROJECTION GAME

It's vital that the audience can hear you at all times. Even if they decide to go to the toilet, or perhaps to the shop to buy some cigarettes during the show. That's why we must constantly be working on our projection.

Get an acting buddy and go out for the day, armed with some scripts. Start by going to a park and standing ten feet apart. Read the scripts aloud, making sure you can hear each other. Now increase the distance. Twenty feet. Fifty feet. A hundred feet. The more people there are in between you, the better. That way not only are you setting yourselves a tougher challenge, but you're also entertaining people who most likely have very little culture in their lives.

Now you need to make things even more difficult. You should be learning to deal with different acoustics, different environments. Go on a bus. One of you stand on the top deck, one of you on the bottom. Project your speeches over the sounds

TOP TIP!
Highlighting your lines with a highlighter pen is a good way of letting the other actors know you don't care about their dialogue

of the bus engine and the passengers' conversations. Go on a tube train. Sit in different carriages. Shout your dialogue over all the sounds around you and see if you can hear each other.

Get creative. Go to as many different places as you can. Go to a city farm and see if you can project over the cacophony of animal noises. Go to a mosque during Friday prayers and see if you can hear each other over the worshipers. Go to a football match, sit in different stands and fire out Shakespeare speeches over the crowd noise. The supporters will, I can guarantee you, love it!

THE UNDERWEAR SHARING GAME

As actors, we are thrown into situations in which we have to pretend to be in close relationships with people we have only just met. The only way to fake the closeness a real-life couple has is to aggressively accelerate the 'getting to know you' process.

Spend a week wearing the same underwear, at the same time. Do everything you would normally do but do it together. Go to the shops, to your sister's wedding, to your Gambler's Anonymous meeting. Before long you'll be completely comfortable in each other's company.

GUIDE DOGS

Before we can perform together we need to trust each other. We need to be able to work as a team. This is a fantastic game for developing a strong working relationship.

First, flip a coin to decide who will be 'blind' and who will be 'dog'. Ok? Great. Now whoever was selected to be blind must put on a blindfold. If you happen to already be blind then you probably don't need to worry about that. Then, whoever was selected as 'dog' must get onto all fours. For the next six weeks, 'dog' will guide 'blind' in everything they do.

I can't recommend this game enough. In fact, I've found it to be a great tool in my everyday life. For the first year of my marriage, in an attempt to start things off on a good footing, we played 'guide dogs'. I spent the first six months as 'blind' and then, halfway through the year, we switched and I became 'dog'. Sadly, the marriage ended within a week or two of the year coming to a close. Do I think that playing 'guide dogs' was the reason for the marriage's failure? The answer to that would have to be a categorical 'no'.

HECKLER

This is a game you can play to support your peers in the industry by keeping them on their toes. Go to a show, sit in the audience and when you feel the time is right, shout out intense criticism…

'I don't believe you!'

'We've all seen that kind of shit a million times before!'

'Your accent is diabolical!'

'Why do you keep doing the same gesture?'

'You're not a credible villain!'

'I've seen better Prospero's done in fucking homeless shelters!'

'When's the interval?'

'Was that meant to be a pause, or did you just forget your line? BECAUSE IT LOOKED LIKE YOU FORGOT YOUR LINE!'

By doing this you are doing the cast a great service for which they will be grateful. Being in a show can get very repetitive and many actors get too comfortable. By heckling them you are shaking things up a bit and giving them a new situation they have to respond to.

I never go to a play without heckling at least once and I am probably really respected in the business for this, I reckon.

BABY TIME

Study after study shows that human beings become the person they are during infancy. When approaching a character it is vital that you don't ignore their formative years.

In order that you can play a character at the age of 35 or whatever, you must, simply *must* spend at least a couple of weeks being that character as a baby. It is helpful to have a partner for this exercise but if you don't just ask to stay at the director's house. They will have the responsibility of feeding, bathing and changing you. You will have the far more difficult responsibility of exploring the first few months of that character's life.

AMBITIOUS BOOK LOVERS

If there's a Spotlight Directory in the audition waiting room, go through it and deface all pictures of actors who look like you. You should always be looking for ways to clamp down on the competition.

FIRE DRILL

All buildings should have a fire drill every week and theatres are no exception. Unfortunately most theatres save their drills for a convenient moment and not during the show. Fire isn't convenient – it's lethal!

Pick a scene that you're not in. I like to choose one which has been going down well with the audience, making the actors a little cocky. Now smash the fire alarm. If the actors aren't still in character at the assembly point then it is *they* who have spoilt it for the audience and *you* have taught them a valuable lesson.

TOP TIP!
NEVER EVER GIVE UP.
Even if you're dog shit at acting and not really that into it

WHAT A BUZZ!

This is a great game for building cast morale. Each night spike a different cast member's drink with ecstasy. Then halfway through the show they'll get a sudden rush of endorphins which they will attribute to the thrill of live performance. I did this to Helen Mirren once in a production of *Death of a Salesman*. It is true that her euphoric final scene as Linda Loman wasn't entirely consistent with the mood of the piece but it was just a delight to see her enjoying herself.

SLOW RUN

Many companies will do a speed run of the play before an important performance – just to make sure everyone knows their lines and is on the ball. That's all very well but it does have a tendency to make actors forget all the in-depth work they've done on subtext and intentions.

A 'slow run' is just as valuable an exercise as a speed one. Simply go through the play as slowly as it is physically possible to do. When I was in a production of *Hamlet* a few years back the time it took up did lead us to only being able to do two performances a week but I can tell you it was well worth it.

ZIP ZAP BOING BONK DING ZING CRUNCH DOOP PING WIGGLE BANG TOMATO

This is the more complicated parent to the popular warm-up game 'Zip Zap Boing'. If you're not familiar with 'Zip Zap Boing' the rules are simple. The actors stand in a circle. Someone says 'zip' to the person to the left of them. The group continue to go round the circle unless someone says 'zap' in which case they go to the right, or 'boing' in which case they point at someone who must then carry on with the game.

Supposedly this is enough to get people warmed up but I think it's far too easy. 'Zip zap boing bonk ding zing crunch doop ping wiggle bang tomato' has a more advanced set of instructions. I will be setting the rules out in their entirety in my forthcoming book; *Zip zap boing bonk ding zing crunch doop ping wiggle bang tomato: a Basic Guide*. To whet your appetite I can tell you that my favourite instruction involves the cast having to commandeer a boat.

GETTING TO KNOW YOU

For a cast to work together successfully it is vital that they get to know one another. Telling each other about our lives and our families is all very well but as artists I feel we really should be going deeper. Much deeper.

We actors are so giving of ourselves that when it comes to being open with our cast mates we have nothing left to give. Pair up with whoever you work closest with in the production and give each other a prostate examination. They say the route to a man's heart is through his stomach. Well, the way to an actor's soul is through their back passage. Get right in there. Explore every crevice. I guarantee you that you will feel a closeness which can only benefit the production.

Are you still inside them? Do you feel you know them a little better than before? Great. Now, don't take it out just yet. Do some of your dialogue together. You should be noticing a difference. It's hard to put your finger on it, but somehow this doesn't quite feel like the last time you ran the scene does it? *That's a good thing.*

Now that you have this exercise, it's there for you whenever you need it. If you ever feel that your scenes are getting a little flat, you know what to do – go fetch those surgical gloves.

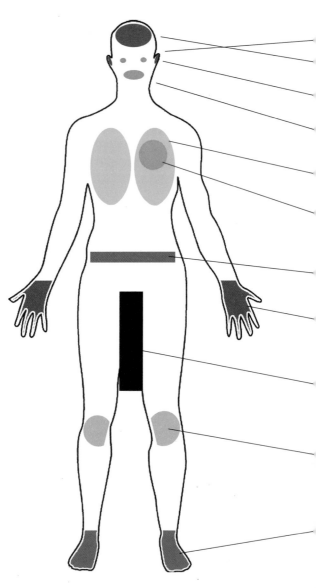

EYES - AN AWFUL LOT OF ACTING IS DONE WITH THE EYES. THIS IS WHY SO FEW ACTORS DON'T HAVE THEM.

BRAIN - WHERE LINES ARE STORED. THIS IS WHY GOOD ACTORS OFTEN HAVE 'BIG HEADS'.

EARS - AN ACTOR MUST ALWAYS BE LISTENING. IT'S ESPECIALLY ENJOYABLE FOR AN ACTOR TO LISTEN TO THE SOUND OF THEIR OWN VOICE.

MOUTH - WHERE DIALOGUE IS TRADITIONALLY SAID FROM.

LUNGS - BREATH, SO IMPORTANT IN THEATRE WORK, COMES FROM HERE. IF YOU STRUGGLE WITH THIS IT CAN BE WORTH INVESTING IN A THIRD LUNG.

HEART - ACTORS HAVE AN ENORMOUS CAPACITY TO FEEL. THIS IS WHY OUR HEARTS ARE THREE TIMES BIGGER THAN NORMAL PEOPLE'S.

WAIST - IF THIS GOES ABOVE 36 INCHES YOU WILL AUTOMATICALLY BE CATEGORISED AS A 'CHARACTER ACTOR'.

HANDS - FOR GESTURING. MAKE SURE EACH WORD IS ACCOMPANIED BY ITS OWN INDIVIDUAL GESTURE.

PENIS - JEWS RUN HOLLYWOOD. IF IT'S NOT ALREADY, IT'S WORTH GETTING THIS CIRCUMCISED TO SHOW SOLIDARITY.

DIAPHRAGM - VOICE COACHES ALWAYS SAY YOU SHOULD SPEAK FROM THE DIAPHRAGM BUT NOT EVERYONE KNOWS WHERE IT IS. IT'S HERE.

FOOT - YOUR AIM IS TO GET THIS IN THE DOOR. MAKE SURE IT'S WELL PEDICURED FOR WHEN YOU EVENTUALLY DO

AFTER-SHOW TIPS

Ok. So you've made people re-evaluate their petty little civilian lives with your stunning performance. What now? The thought that someone might see you leave in the same clothes you arrived in is too harrowing to contemplate so get out of your costume and step into your evening wear. But don't leave just yet. The chances are you have an army of autograph hunters at stage door. Make them wait. Even if it's not the case you should at least give the illusion that it takes you a little while to shake off the character, so leave it a while. I recommend about 30-45 minutes.

Now put on some dark glasses and an 'I'm too good for this air' and go and sign some programmes. Here, you want to give off the impression that although you value the support of your public, far too much of your time is taken up by signing autographs. When thinking about an appropriate approach to this vital part of an actor's life I have taken a lot from the way in which tennis players sign autographs after their matches. The quicker and less legible your autograph is – the bigger the star you are. I recommend going for a tiny single dot. Trust me – just the fact that that dot was created by the hand of a real-life semi-professional actor will be enough to keep the recipient in wet dreams for months.

The way you handle the whole post-show stage door situation will of course depend somewhat on the level of your fame. If you have stalkers, for example, your aim should be not to allow them to come too close whilst at the same time giving them just enough encouragement to remain your stalker. When you're going through hard times the

TOP TIP!
The bow is a good opportunity to shout 'Fuck you Dad! I told you I could do it! I'm a fucking actor Dad!'

existence of a stalker is a valuable self-esteem booster so don't take them for granted. I had a stalker once whom I neglected. Before I knew it she'd given up on me and moved onto bigger and better things in the form of the almighty Ralf Little. So feed your stalker's interest with the odd smile but hugs are a no no.

If you don't have a stalker, you really need to get one. Pay a Polish immigrant or something if needs be.

Now for a much-needed drink. You have just been working for an hour and forty-five minutes after all. You deserve one. Your first bar needs to be one containing as many audience members from your show as possible. This gives you the best chance of getting compliments and, if you're lucky, free drinks. But you won't get either of those if no one notices you so make sure they do. Immediately look for a fellow cast member and shout their name across the room making it clear you've just been in the play...

'DEBORAH! OR SHOULD I SAY JULIET?! FEAR NOT, YOUR ROMEO IS HERE!'

Then go straight into a hearty actory laugh to show how much fun you are off stage.

If you had a smaller part it might take a bit more work to get people to recognise you as a member of the company. Wear one part of your costume, as if you've just forgotten to take it off. Something simple like a sword or a codpiece. You know, something that won't make you look silly but still says 'I was in the play'.

If a compliment is not immediately forthcoming, do a few laps of the room, maybe humming a song from the show or just mumbling your lines. Make your face open and approachable and try to look anyone you can in the eye. If and when a stranger does compliment you on the show say the following line…

'Thanks very much but no I'm ok.'

That should confuse them a little. Then say…

'Oh sorry. I thought you offered to buy me a drink. My mistake.'

They most likely will offer to buy you a drink out of awkwardness. Then say…

'Oh fine. If you absolutely insist. I'll have a Grey Goose martini with a twist please. Thank you.'

As soon as you've got the drink, pretend to get a phone call and disappear.

You are unlikely to have to work quite so hard to get compliments if you have friends in. In fact, if a friend comes to see your show and the first thing that comes out of their mouth isn't 'Well done. You were great,' you are well within your rights to disown them. Unless you've chosen your friends horrifically poorly that won't be the case. So how do you respond when they do give you the obligatory compliment? Every actor in the world knows the answer to that question so it seems too obvious to put it in writing. I am willing to accept though that this book may have somehow fallen into the hands of a layperson. So here it is. When a friend compliments an actor on a live performance they have just seen them give, the actor must always reply with the following words…

'Oh, really? We felt it was a bit flat tonight actually.'

If only every sentence could be so perfect. It does so much in so little time. With a simple economical elegance it suits your purposes no matter what your friend is thinking. If they were lying and actually thought the show or you were bad then it's a ready-made excuse. They will go away thinking 'Oh well, I guess we just saw an off-night'. If they genuinely thought you were good then it leaves them to think 'Wow! Just imagine how fantastic they must be on a night that isn't flat!'.

Now, because your friends have just come to see you perform, you have a great opportunity to talk about yourself for a good few hours. Don't worry, assuming they're not actors themselves, they won't mind at all. Those precious moments when they get to hear about you are probably the greatest thing in their lives. Talk in great detail about the rehearsal process and how you approached the role. Then show you're interested in what they have to say by asking them questions about the show…

'Who do you think was the worst actor?'

'Could you hear the girl playing Olivia?… Yeah, I thought not. I think she went to a northern drama school.'

'If you had arranged the curtain call would you have put me closer to the centre?'

Then, if you're feeling generous, finish off the night by taking your friends to a karaoke room and treating them to a couple of hours of you singing show tunes.

ACCENTS

There is no doubting the fact that the ability to do accents is likely to increase your chances of getting work. If Tom Cruise and Nicole Kidman couldn't do authentic Irish accents do you really think they would have been cast in *Far and Away*? Of course not.

If you really want to show off your versatility, one technique I highly recommend is to do a different accent in every scene. In fact far too many actors pay credence to the idea that consistency of character is a virtue when it comes to acting. I disagree. If the audience have seen you have a limp in one scene, don't bore them with it in the next scene. Shake things up! Scrap the limp and introduce a new defect. Maybe a lisp or a violent tick. Every role is an opportunity to display as many of your skills as possible.

My low-life publisher seems to think that it will be difficult for me to teach accents in writing. He thinks that an audio tape or video would be a better medium for such a lesson. He is wrong and I'm about to prove it…

The three main accents are received pronunciation, American and working class but I'm going to go a little deeper. Let's start with…

'SCOTCH'

Scottish, or as all Scottish people call it, Scotch is a difficult accent to crack. This is because if you're not from Scotland you probably don't have the same level of violent aggression genetically stored within you. Let's start with a phrase the average Scot or 'Scotch' uses five or six times a day…

'Say one more word and I'll put your head through this fucking giant iron spike I carry around with me at all times'.

Ok. The quickest way to get yourself to the point where you can casually spout such threatening bile is to go to prison. Get convicted of a crime that will see you locked up for about three months – burglary or moderate arson should do the trick. Befriend your fellow inmates by telling them that you're an actor. Maybe perform a monologue or two for them. Perhaps something light-hearted from *Taming of the Shrew*. Then immerse yourself in the culture. You'll come out a battle-hardened beast ready to say that phrase in authentic Scotch…

'See wun murr wurd end all pit yurr heed thrur dis fookin jant irin spuck ah curry arrund worth mu ut ell toms.'

PERFECT.

'GEORDIE'

This accent is spoken by the inhabitants of a city in the north of England called 'Newcastle'. Thanks to a good education and a strong moral upbringing I have never actually been to Newcastle but I do know how to do the accent. The first thing you need to do is get yourself into the mindset of a Geordie. Do something a Geordie would do. I recommend eating a sausage roll for breakfast. Then think about trying out a sentence. Here's a common Geordie phrase…

> **'I'm so tired from working down the grease factory that I forgot to bring home some ale and pork scratchings for our tea'.**

After a week of sausage roll breakfasts and sink washes that phrase should start to come out of your mouth like this…

> **'Amm su tured frum wurkin doon da greash foctory dat ah forgutt tu brong humm soom all und purk scrutchins fur urr tah'.**

Read that sentence out loud. There you have it. PERFECT Geordie.

'FRENCH'

This one is easy. Just say 'uhhh' before every third word. PERFECT.

LIVERPOOL, OR 'SCOUSE'

Be careful with this one. If you don't stretch properly you could easily give yourself a serious injury. The defining feature of the 'scouse' accent is the way in which they say their hard Cs or Ks. Let me give you an example.

The word 'back' becomes: bakkkkkhhhhhh!

The word 'romantic' becomes: romantikkkkkkhhhh!

The only way to achieve this is by preparing to spit at the back of your throat. It's disgusting, I know, but if TV producers are going to insist on putting these types of people on television I'm afraid we're going to have to learn their ways.

AUSTRALIAN

This is essentially just shouting.

NORTHERN IRISH

This is the most terrifying accent known to man. Like with Australian, you will need to shout but this time imagine the sound of your voice is being filtered through an angry cheese grater.

Now read this chapter three more times and you will have every accent you'll ever need at your disposal.

LETTER TO A CASTING DIRECTOR

The following is a template for a letter I send to every casting director about once every two weeks. Since first sending it out in 1998 I have had somewhere in the region of eleven auditions. I have now decided to give this powerful document to you.

Casting directors receive literally billions of letters from actors every day. Well aware of this fact, I have endeavoured to make mine stand out in the opening paragraph and grab their attention. I then go on to make some moderate exaggerations about my acting experience. ALL ACTORS LIE. IT'S OUR JOB. DON'T BE THE IDIOT WHO DOESN'T.

TOP TIP!
If you want casting directors to watch the whole thing, your showreel should be no longer than 6 hours

Please note – it wasn't until 2005 that I realised I had been forgetting to replace 'insert name' with the actual relevant names. Don't make the same mistake I did.

Dear (insert name),

I've been watching you for some time. I like the way you move. I like the way you operate. I like the way you find a perfect balance between your work life and your family life.

And, may I say, what a wonderful family you appear to have. There's just one thing missing in your life… me.

Hi. My name is (insert name) and I am an actor who is writing to you in the hope that you might like to see me for a casting at some point. You may have seen my work before. As well as extensive work in the voluntary theatre field I was one of Biff's gang in the *Back to the Future* trilogy and for the last 20 years have played Ian Beale in EastEnders.

If you are casting anything you feel I may be suitable for (I can play black) I would love to meet you. I can come to your office or if it's easier for you I'd be happy to meet you at your house. For your convenience, for the next week I will be at the bottom of your driveway between the hours of 7 a.m. and 10 a.m. and if you would like to see me just pop down and invite me in.

I look forward to meeting you soon.

(insert name)

BONUS TIP!
This is an arresting letter but on its own it might not be enough. Why not make it stand out even more by adding perfume and glitter glue?

JOBS IN ORDER OF THEIR VALUE TO SOCIETY...

1. Actor

2. Doctor

3. Dresser

4. Firefighter

5. (Drama) Teacher

6. Street performer

7. Nurse

8. Theatre usher

9. Agent

10. Director

LOOK LIKE YOU KNOW WHAT YOU'RE DOING

Far more important than knowing what you're doing is looking like you know what you're doing. Whenever you are on set, in rehearsal or doing a pre-show warm-up you are being judged by other actors. They are trying to figure out if you're just a charlatan, playing at being an actor.

TOP TIP!
You need to be in character from your head to your toes. If a part of your body isn't, hide it behind a prop

One of the best ways of appearing like the real deal is with a loud and complex-sounding vocal warm-up. Just walk around the back stage, your dressing room, the theatre bar, doing random sounds at the top of your voice:

BAAAAAAA! MOOOOOOO! FEEEEEEE CRRRAAAAAAABBBBBB!

Intersperse them with lines of dialogue. Shout those lines in an odd, deliberate way:

'THE. THEEEEE. MASTER'S. MAAAAAASSSSSTTTTTEEERRR'S. HORSE. HOOOORRRRRSSSSEEEE. IS READY SIR. READY! READY! THE MASTER'S HORSE IS READY. REEEEAAADDDDYYY SIR.'

As long as you do all of that with a stern face which implies it's all very worthwhile you'll look like a professional. It will, of course, have zero effect on your performance but that's not what matters.

Here are some other ways you can look like you know what you're doing…

1. **Ask the cameraman what size shot they're doing of you. The answer isn't likely to change your performance in any way but it sounds like the sort of thing an experienced actor would ask.**

2. **Walk around with a copy of Stanislavski's *An Actor Prepares* at all times. Note: there is absolutely no requirement to actually read it. No one does.**

3. **Ask the director questions like 'Do you want me to dial up the subtext in this scene, or just let it simmer?'. The director, just like you, wants to look like they know what they're doing so will go along with it. Even though you'll both be talking utter bollocks.**

4. **Throw in the odd bit of jargon like 'It's been a while since I've worked on a thrust stage,' or 'What time is the two shot?'.**

5. **If a line in the script is in italics, it means you should be leaning when you say it.**

6. Take your GCSE Drama certificate (or whatever your country's equivalent is) to all auditions.

7. Constantly criticise other actors' performances. After the director gives their notes – give yours!

8. When the make-up artist asks if you're allergic to anything, always say 'yes' and make something up.

9. During the read-through of a Shakespeare script, laugh loudly at random moments. It makes it look like you know what's going on.

10. Say things like 'I never really feel I know my character until I've found the right shoes'. Shit like that.

TOP TIP!
If you feel the director is spending too much time working on other actors' scenes – fake an asthma attack

METHOD ACTING

The principals behind method acting are simple. In order to portray an emotion we have to experience that emotion ourselves. For example – instead of pretending to get shot in the chest, a method actor *will* get shot in the chest.

Invented by the US military during the Korean War, to give troops the grittier entertainment they longed for, method acting has become popular with modern audiences and actors alike.

Some of the most well-known exponents include Dustin Hoffman, Daniel Day-Lewis and Adam Woodyatt aka Ian Beale from EastEnders. If the character, Ian Beale, is drinking tea in the scene then the actor, Adam Woodyatt, is drinking tea. Not hot chocolate. Not coffee. TEA.

> ## INTERESTING FACT!
> When I die I'm donating my body to actors researching the role of 'Surgeon'

Method acting was perhaps first popularised by the late, great weight Marlon Brando. Throughout his career Brando would astonish his fellow actors with the dedication he gave to each role. Before playing Superman's father in the 1978 movie he spent six months living on a failed makeshift Krypton. Brando paid some out-of-work Native Americans to build him the dummy Krypton in the Arizona desert out of paper mache and Cherokee wisdom. Quickly the fake planet burnt under the midday sun but the stubborn Brando insisted on living on the ashes that remained, frequently shouting 'I am Jor-El, Superman's father, and if I say this is Krypton then this is Krypton!'.

Christopher Reeve looked up to Brando so much that later in life he tried to persuade Marlon that his now paralysed state was intentional research for his TV remake of *Rear Window*. By this stage though, Brando was so engrossed in his own long-term research for the role of a chronically obese person that he didn't notice. Sadly Brando died before he could ever shoot the movie and his role in *Precious* was instead played by Gabourey Sidibe.

And what of you? I urge you to be careful when dipping your emotional toe into the choppy waters of 'the method'. DANGER! DANGER! DON'T STAND TOO CLOSE TO THE EDGE! By all means 'go method' but take it slowly. Playing a murderer? Don't, for heaven's sake, go around murdering people. Not unless you have training. Not yet. Start by doing things that help to get you into the mindset of a murderer. Maybe dodge a train fare, miscalculate a restaurant bill in your favour, throw a barbed comment at a tramp. Though not actual 'murder' per se, each of these acts can get you 'in the right place'.

Still not feeling it? Ok. You're going to have to do a murder. Yes, someone's going to get hurt but that's not for you to worry about. The most important thing to any actor must, simply MUST be the production they are preparing for. That and the standard of the decor in the green room. HA! ACTOR'S JOKE! No, in all seriousness the production is *numero uno* (number one).

First. Go back to the script and ask yourself 'do I really need to do this?'. If your character simply says 'I could murder a cup of coffee' then you probably don't need to murder a person. Murdering a cup of coffee will do. But if your character has indeed murdered a human being then you need to select a victim.

I'll leave it up to you to select the person you feel whose life is worth sacrificing in the name of drama. It's no use murdering another actor. Whilst gaining a more layered performance from yourself you could be robbing us of another fine performance in the future. Murder someone like a cleaner or a labourer or a teacher. Someone who won't be missed.

REMEMBER! DON'T GET CAUGHT! If you're in prison while the production's on then you're no good to anyone.

Have you done it yet? Ok. Great. Do you feel in character yet? If so, fantastic. If not, don't worry. Not everything works. The research and rehearsal process is about experimentation. There's no point fretting over something that's been and gone. At least you tried. Now, good luck with your *Chitty Chitty Bang Bang* production.

WHAT TO WEAR

How you dress, in rehearsals, auditions or just in your everyday life, will affect the way that you are perceived. It is vital that you fit into one of the acceptable 'actor's attire' categories.

YOUNG, INTERESTING MALE ACTOR

Tight v-neck T-shirt. Black jeans. Bare feet.

MALE ACTOR IN FORTIES WHO WANTS TO MAINTAIN EDGE

Leather jacket. Cowboy boots. Enter rehearsal room carrying motorcycle helmet – no need to actually ride a motorbike. Always smoke roll-ups.

MALE ACTOR IN 50s/60s WHO WANTS TO BELIEVE THEY CAN HAVE SEX WITH FRONT OF HOUSE STAFF

Shirt with at least six buttons undone revealing white but sexy chest hair. Reading glasses in top pocket. One pirate-style hooped earring. Big wooly rehearsal room socks which say, 'Look, I've been doing this a long time and I know what the fuck I'm doing'. Copy of the *Guardian* under their arm.

MALE ACTOR/ACTRESS
WHO DOESN'T WORK MUCH

T-shirt from show they've been in before to make people think they have worked a lot.

YOUNG SERIOUS ACTRESS

Black leggings. Black vest with moderate cleavage. Bottle of Evian. Salad.

YOUNG MUSICAL ACTRESS

Black leggings. Brightly coloured vest revealing a bit more cleavage. Bigger bottle of Evian. Bigger salad.

ACTRESS OVER FORTY

Big shawl/indoor scarf which they got from Nepal. Ethnic earrings. Home-made lentil juice. Tupperware box of seeds. Vegan rehearsal shoes. Arrive everywhere ten minutes late in a green mini.

FOOD TIPS

It is an unfortunate truth that your appearance will have more of an effect on the success or failure of your career than anything else. Do you honestly think that Steve Buscemi would have got where he is today if he hadn't been blessed with his dazzling good looks? This is why it is essential that you treat your body like a temple. That is unless you get a lot of work playing fat characters – in which case don't worry about it.

Here is a list of the only foods an actor is allowed to eat…

SEEDS Emotionally fragile actresses in particular love seeds and who can blame them? With as little as half a calorie in each seed you can afford to eat ten in one sitting and not feel guilty about the bottle of Evian you have for dessert.

RICE CAKES This food has the word 'cake' in it so it *has* to be delicious. All real actresses carry a packet of rice cakes around in their bag at all times. That means they are always ready to take a bite

TOP TIP!
Combine your seed eating habits with animal work by pecking your meal out of a bird feeder

and do the whole 'I can't stop eating these. I'm such a pig and yet I'm so skinny!' thing.

CARROT STICKS Not only are these low in calories and therefore 'actor edible' but they also help you see in the dark. This comes in handy when leaving stage during a blackout.

BEANS AND PULSES These are (probably) high in fibre. They are also very good at saying 'I have a low income because I choose to only do worthy theatre to small uninterested audiences in rural arts centres'.

ANYTHING FROM A CINEMA Although not necessarily healthy this is good on two counts. Firstly, if you're a film actor, eating the food of the movie-going public allows you to relate to your audience and understand them for who they are – filthy under-nourished slobs. Secondly, since you can prove this food was bought on a 'research trip' to the cinema, it's tax deductible. Between 2005 and 2008, every single meal I ate was at the cinema. If you think that means my diet lacked variety you'd be wrong. For breakfast I'd usually go with ice cream. The wide range of flavours meant I never got bored. Lunch tended to be nachos and dinner was either two hot dogs or a large popcorn mixed with fruit pastilles for the vitamins. Dessert was £5 worth of pick 'n mix (avoiding fudge which is deceivingly heavy), washed down with a large Sprite. I'm not afraid to say that food-wise they were the happiest three years of my life.[*] The only thing that ended it was that the high salt intake meant my liver stopped functioning. I also realised that the high prices outweighed any benefit I was getting through tax deductibility. That false economy was one of the major factors in my 2009 bankruptcy. Still, no regrets. I look back on those days very fondly and think of them every time I have a difficult bowel movement.

---

[*] Relationship-wise they were difficult years. There are only so many films on at the cinema at any one time and having three meals a day there meant I had to watch most films five or six times. It was nigh on impossible to find anyone who would watch films such as *Spy Kids Two* so frequently and I will admit to becoming severely lonely during this period. Like I say though – no regrets.

CORPSING TIPS

Giggling during a performance is known in the industry as 'corpsing'. This is because in the days of Shakespeare, an actor who laughed when they weren't supposed to was taken outside and murdered by the assistant director – thereby turning them into a 'corpse'. In the same way that the end of corporal punishment in schools brought about a deterioration in standards of pupil behaviour, the banning of killing bad actors has led to an increase in corpsing.

Don't let yourself become one of these guffawing low-lifes. The best way to avoid it is by taking your craft the way it's supposed to be taken – seriously. Stay away from any actors who seem to be enjoying themselves. These people are hedonist buffoons who will no doubt be dead before they're thirty.

Everyone makes at least one mistake in their life though[*] and you may find yourself in the middle of a performance and feel that you're about to laugh. If, God forbid, this does happen turn to the audience and apologise…

'I am ashamed to say that I was about to laugh and thereby tarnish this evening's performance irreparably. So that you get the show that you deserve we will now begin the play from the beginning'.

---

[*] Mine was punching Trevor Nunn.

I heard of a case in which somebody began to laugh in the final speech of *Hamlet* and the show was restarted. This led to the evening becoming eight hours long but it was *the right thing to do.*

OPINION!
It takes great courage to stand on a stage and act. That's why the kids who are into drama tend to be the toughest in the school

IT'S NEVER TOO LATE TO BE A CHILD ACTOR

Let's get something out of the way immediately. Ninety per cent of child actors are actually adults. People wonder how Natalie Portman in *Leon*, Hayley Joel Osment in *The Sixth Sense* or Rudy Huxtable in *The Cosby Show* gave such powerful performances at such a young age. The answer is they didn't. They were all in their thirties at the time.

But how did they appear so young? Make-up? Camera trickery? No. Each of those performers was able to appear so young thanks to the use of the greatest trick of all... acting. Once you become a truly great actor (and you will by the end of this book) you will develop the power to act yourself into appearing younger or older. The only reason the make-up department on *The Curious Case of Benjamin Button* won an Oscar is because Brad Pitt was too humble to admit that he actually did all of his aging through pure unadulterated acting. Here's one for you – the finest performance I have ever seen was from Al Pacino in *The Godfather: Part II*. People say the first time Pacino and Robert De Niro were ever together on screen was in the movie *Heat*. It wasn't. It was when Pacino played Michael Corleone as a baby and De Niro held him in his arms in *The Godfather: Part II*.

So what are the advantages of being a child actor? Well, once you have mastered the skill of making yourself appear like a child the job is actually quite easy. For a child to simply remember and then say a line is always considered cute. In fact if you mess up a line, as long as the audience believes that you actually are a child you'll be considered even cuter. Then if you show any kind of emotion or timing people will say that you're incredible. Until the year 2000 Dakota Fanning was a very average actress in her early forties whose career was going nowhere. Then she learnt how to 'play child' and suddenly she was getting all the praise in the world.

So how do you do it? How do you act yourself into looking like a child? Start out by absorbing yourself into a child's environment. Go to a local park and spend as much time as you can with children, doing the things that children do. Go on the slide. Play on the swings. Talk to the other children in a kiddy voice. A concerned parent may ask you what you're doing. Calmly explain to them (whilst maintaining the infant voice) that you are an actor researching a role. They will understand.

Once you've done this for ten hours every day for about six months you should begin to feel like a child. If you've really been working yourself into character just by the sheer force of the wondrous thing we call 'acting' you should be starting to look like a child. Now it's time to test it out. Walk into a local primary school and try and get yourself enrolled there.

Are you in? Yes? Congratulations. You're ready to be a child actor. Now get yourself in a school play, invite a load of casting directors and wait for the offers to roll in.

LETTER TO A FORMER TEACHER

You didn't become an actor by accident. The chances are that at some point in your life a drama teacher inspired you. I think it is important to thank that person for where you are today. Here is a template for a letter you can send...

Dear (insert name),

I would like to think that you haven't forgotten me but if it's not immediately apparent let me rekindle your memory. (insert number) years ago I was your keenest student and thanks to the passion you instilled in me I went on to pursue a career in acting.

Without your inspirational lessons my life could have been so different. Right now I would most likely be living in a three-bedroomed house with a family and a boring steady job. Instead, I chose to follow my dreams meaning I never know what I'll be doing from week to week. It's so exciting! One week I'm temping at some council offices, the next I'm temping at an insurance firm.

I still use everything you taught me all the time. The work you did on my diction has helped me when temping at innumerable call centres and I don't know how I would have got through some of my data entry stints without your teachings on focussing.

I do hope we bump into each other again some time, but if not perhaps you'll be seeing me on television. I had an audition for a Lawyers4U commercial last year and am yet to hear back. No news is good news!

I'm sorry this letter can't be longer but I am on my break at the potato peeling factory I am currently temping at and the bell to go back to work has just rung. Let me just finish by saying that I will never forget the words you said to me…

'I believe in you. You can make it.'

Thank you so much. I feel that every day I am getting closer.

Signed

(insert name)

SHARED DRESSING ROOM TIPS

One of the greatest travesties in the world today is that some actors are still having to go through the indignity of sharing a dressing room. The fact that I've never seen a newspaper run a piece on this ongoing injustice just goes to show what an oppressed minority us actors are.

I've heard of instances where actors are packed four, even five to a room with only three dressers between them. That can't be right. Amnesty International seem to be dragging their heels on this issue so it's up to us to fight it. I urge you to write to your MP or Congressperson and demand action. Until the day comes when each actor has the dressing room they deserve we, like the victims of Apartheid, suffrage and serfdom before us, will have to learn to cope.

If you find yourself in such circumstances, the first thing you need to do is put your own personal imprint on the culture of the room. I like to sit my room-mates down immediately and set out some ground rules. The first and most important rule is <u>No Joking</u>. Acting is a serious business. As soon as I arrive at the theatre I am there to work. Any jokes made by other actors will only distract me. The theatre is not a place of fun. It is a place of concentration, a place of art, a place of *Dirty Dancing: The Musical* or whatever show you're in.

For men especially, the smell can become a serious problem. With so much sweat and so many costume changes the stench can become overpowering. I insist that rather than attempting to combat it with deodorants and the like that we embrace it and use it to our advantage. That stench is a mark of our toil in the name of art and a reminder of the toil we still have to do. That stench is inspirational. It is an absolute non-negotiable for me that no actor who shares a dressing room with me may wash themselves or their costume during the run of a show.

Here's a list of the rest of my dressing room rules…

1. **No talking before the show. It puts me off. We're here to work.**

2. **I'm allowed to talk. Sorry, if that seems unfair. It's just how I warm up.**

3. **Always be on alert, in case I decide to start a game of zip zap boing.**

4. **No smiling. It puts me off.**

5. **Have fun!**

WAYS TO MAKE YOUR SPOTLIGHT PHOTO STAND OUT

1. Create an air of irresistible mystery around you by not turning up to the photo shoot and simply having an empty chair.

2. Demonstrate your emotional range – if you're not crying in your photo then how are they supposed to know you can do it?

3. Go to a caricature artist and use their drawing of you.

4. Get more roles as villains by using a mug shot.

5. No one will forget a photo of a white person racistly dressed up as a Chinese person.

6. Hypnotise them into hiring you by photoshopping your eyes into spirals.

7. If you're holding an Oscar in your headshot they'll think you must have won one. They won't be bothered to check. Trust me.

8. Short? Make them think you're taller by having your head above frame.

9. Show how relaxed you are by picking your nose in it.

10. Have a thought bubble coming from your head saying 'Boy, do I love to act?!'

11. Remind them of what you've been in by having your CV tattooed to your face.

12. Look cool by having a cigarette hanging out of your mouth.

13. Show you're not needy by having your back to the camera.

14. Use a brass rubbing of your face. Trust me – they're coming back in a big way!

15. Use a photo of you with someone famous.

16. Use a photo of a sad child so they at least call you in out of sympathy.

17. Have a large lung capacity? Show them how good your vocal work will be by using an X-ray of your chest.

18. All actors use photos that make themselves look younger. Trump them all by using a baby photo.

19. Be winking in it. Shows your playful sexy side.

20. Have you ever seen a headshot in which the actor is giving the finger? Neither have I. Make yours the first.

SUPERSTITIONS

Many actors have superstitions. For some it's just a little thing they do before they perform. Some cross themselves and say a little prayer, some touch a lucky mascot. One of my own superstitions is to snort a line of cocaine before every scene. Don't ask me why. It's just become something I do for luck and I'd be lost without it. It's got to the stage where I'll even do it when I'm not performing. Before I do the washing up or answer the door. Anything really. We're funny little creatures of habit, us actors.

Probably the most well-known theatrical superstition is to always refer to *Macbeth* as 'The Scottish Play'. The last time anyone did actually say 'Macbeth' out loud in a theatre, 79 audience members, and tragically 2 actors died. The reasons behind this are not really understood. During the Cold War the American military tried to weaponise the word. Undercover agents would infiltrate Russian theatre companies and when the moment was right, say 'Macbeth'. For whatever reason, it just didn't work. My theory is that the Soviet government had found some kind of 'Macbeth' vaccine.

Another popular superstition is to never wish an actor 'good luck'. This stems from the fact that all performers secretly want their peers to fail. The phrase 'good luck' is traditionally replaced with 'break a leg' but I feel that this isn't quite strong enough. These days my choice of phrase is 'contract a deadly disease'.

Anyone who's ever worked in a theatre will know that the vast majority of them are haunted by the ghosts of actors. Bored in the afterlife, these pesky spirits get their kicks from disrupting the performances of the living. I have been plagued by a particularly mischievous ghost for the past fifteen years. Every one of my shows features a mistake of some sort, which I am certain is caused by this bastard. Whether I'm in the theatre, filming TV or even in an audition I will at some point trip over a prop or forget a line and I have no doubt that it's this fucking ghost that's to blame. Now, in every one of my programme entries is a note which explains that I'm acting under a handicap. After my credits it will simply say 'Fergus is haunted by a prankster ghost.' That way the audience can understand that I'm not operating on a level playing field.

INTERESTING FACT!
In the theatre world **Macbeth** must always be referred to as 'the Scottish play' and **Merry Wives of Windsor** as 'the shitty play'

Here are some other superstitions I highly recommend adhering to...

1. **Always steal something from the pockets of every actor you work with.**

2. **Never work with children or animals — unless they have a basic understanding of the Stanislavski process.**

3. **Ward off evil spirits by urinating in all four corners of the stage, your dressing room and your cast mates' dressing rooms.**

4. **Always do your third scene with your back to the audience.**

5. **If you mess up a line — spin round three times and spit in the face of an audience member/cameraman.**

6. **Always enter stage left and exit stage right... no matter what the director says.**

7. **It's bad luck to masturbate during a performance.**

8. **Don't talk to anyone for three hours before every performance.**

9. **Do every seventh scene while standing on one leg.**

10. **It's bad luck not to be centre of the bow.**

POO GUIDE

People are always surprised when they find out that actors go to the toilet. Yes, the things we do are superhuman but that doesn't mean we don't have normal human bodily functions. Traipsing from audition to voiceover to therapist can make it difficult for us to find somewhere to poo. I have been compiling this essential guide to free toilets in London's West End over a number of years. I look forward to sharing a hand dryer with you at one of these venues sometime soon.

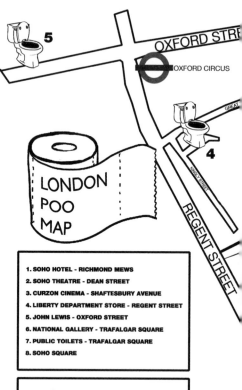

OXFORD STREET

OXFORD CIRCUS

GREAT

REGENT STREET

5

4

LONDON POO MAP

1. SOHO HOTEL - RICHMOND MEWS
2. SOHO THEATRE - DEAN STREET
3. CURZON CINEMA - SHAFTESBURY AVENUE
4. LIBERTY DEPARTMENT STORE - REGENT STREET
5. JOHN LEWIS - OXFORD STREET
6. NATIONAL GALLERY - TRAFALGAR SQUARE
7. PUBLIC TOILETS - TRAFALGAR SQUARE
8. SOHO SQUARE

TOILET

NEAREST TUBE

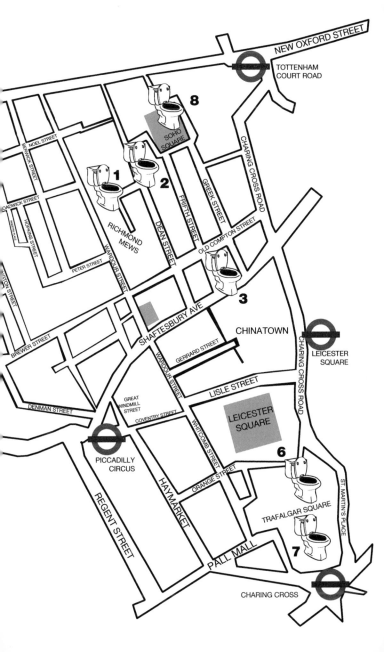

1. SOHO HOTEL – RICHMOND MEWS

Posh hotels are severely underused free toilet facilities. Walk in confidently and you could easily be a hotel guest. Here, you could also be visiting the bar so there is zero chance of you being stopped. Simply walk past the desk, through a couple of doors and into a clean toilet with two rarely used cubicles. The ladies may have more. I don't know. I'm not a pervert. Nice taps and clean hand towels make it a pleasurable experience. Upon leaving you will often receive a 'thank you' from one of the door men. 'Oh, you're welcome. You're very welcome'.

2. SOHO THEATRE – DEAN STREET

Not quite as clean or as quiet as the Soho Hotel but still easily accessible. The mens' only have one cubicle and the lock is temperamental but it's still a solid destination for solid disposal. A massive pro is that upon leaving you may be seen by an old drama school classmate who will assume that you're actually working there.

3. CURZON CINEMA – SHAFTESBURY AVENUE

Way down in the basement, it's a great refuge from the pressures of London life above sea level. Seeing as every film on in there is French it is also unlikely that it will bring on any depression at your not being in them.

4. LIBERTY DEPARTMENT STORE – REGENT STREET

PROS: It's a free and usually quiet toilet in which you can really let rip should that be required.

CONS: It's not easy to find and you will have to walk past a huge amount of things you will never be able to afford on your income which is probably prison workshop-based.

5. JOHN LEWIS – OXFORD STREET

A last resort. Far too popular for my liking and way up on the fifth floor. If you're a man though, it will give you an opportunity to study the role of 'middle aged husband avoiding wife' as these toilets are full of them.

6. NATIONAL GALLERY – TRAFALGAR SQUARE

The most cultured poo you're likely to find. I did for a while think this might be a good place to be seen but the last actor to go in here for anything other than a poo was Laurence Olivier in 1951.

7. PUBLIC TOILETS – TRAFALGAR SQUARE

Yes, I too am repulsed by the word 'public' but they aren't bad. Seeing as almost everyone who uses them are tourists you can kid them into thinking that you're actually really famous in this country. Just have a long imaginary phone conversation with your imaginary agent while you defecate.

8. SOHO SQUARE

Feel that the industry is ignoring you? Pick a sunny July lunchtime to do your business in the middle of Soho Square and they won't be ignoring you anymore. This could be your best chance to get casting directors talking about you.

STAGE PRESENCE

You're in your costume, you know your lines and your voice and body are warmed up to acting mark 6 but there's still something missing – stage presence. Unless you have that indefinable thing we call presence no one is going to look at you.

Some actors have it naturally. In his theatre days Daniel Day-Lewis's stage presence was superhuman. It got to the stage where the play itself was redundant. The rest of the cast stopped bothering coming and Day-Lewis stopped bothering to say the lines. He would simply stand on stage, silent, exuding presence for three hours and the audience would leave saying it was the best thing they had ever seen. In 1986 Loughborough University did an experiment in which they checked to see if DDL's presence could pass through walls. On one side was an audience of about thirty, on the other was Daniel Day-Lewis – in between them… 2 metres of solid concrete.

The results were extraordinary. Yes, Day-Lewis's presence was diluted somewhat but the entire audience said that they felt there was a great actor behind the wall. When DDL walked around the concrete his undiluted presence was enough to physically knock out two people. Since then Day-Lewis has been banned from live performance. On his film sets, for their own safety the crew are asked to put on the same sort of industrial radiation suits that first responders at a nuclear disaster wear.

The likelihood is that you don't have that kind of presence. Fear not! Presence is simply a useful tool to get audiences to look at you instead of the other actors. There are ways you can manufacture that. Every performance is a competition to see who can gain the most attention – here are some tips on how to win that battle…

Let's say you're in a modern production of *Henry V*. You and the other soldiers are all wearing camouflage army fatigues. Unless you're fortunate enough to be the token black actor, it's going to be very difficult for the audience to distinguish you from the other performers. Get creative! Why not sprinkle some glitter over your outfit? Perhaps give your character a tick?

Using your voice is a great way of standing out. Let's stick with the *Henry V* soldier example. Your fellow cast members will, most likely, be going for deep manly voices. This is a great opportunity to make yourself completely recognisable by going full falsetto. Congratulations! You've won! Every one in that audience will remember you.

Some of you may be thinking about the tricky issue of getting this choice past the director. You're right. Most directors are so self-involved that they spend their whole time worrying about 'the play as a whole' and don't think for a second about the biological need actors have for attention. This is why it is vital that you don't introduce your glitter/tick/falsetto until press night.

In your efforts to attract the audience's warming gaze you may encounter a problem – a talented colleague. To be honest unless you're working in the West End or on Broadway this is actually quite unlikely to come up. If it does though, you're going to need to consider sabotage. Give them a chance first though. Knock on their dressing room door and politely ask them to give a slightly worse performance. Explain that it's making you look bad and that for the good of everyone they should sacrifice their own fucking ego and stop showing off.

How did it go? No? Yes, I thought so. Talent and good manners are seldom found in the same person. Alright then. They've brought it on themselves – it's time to start sabotaging their performance.

Confidently feed them the wrong lines. You will look like you know exactly what you're doing and they will be utterly lost. Let's say they're playing Hamlet. Five or six lines into the 'To be or not to be' speech run in and shout – 'My Lord! News from Rome! The general's army are headed northwards!'.

If they clam up then you've won on three counts: 1. you've got an extra line; 2. you've made them look bad; and 3. in turn, you've made yourself look good. Win. Win. Win. If they handle it well by neatly improvising around your interjection then hats off to them. They're quite the actor. Any ill feeling between you can be sorted afterwards over a refreshing Tia Maria in the theatre bar.

BEING A REBEL

Since acting began as a parlour game in upper-class Victorian Britain one thing has remained a constant – rebels. There is something about the rebel actor that has always been appealing to audiences. From Oliver Reed's drunken talk show appearances to Sean Penn sending Osama bin Laden to collect his Oscar, being a renegade has always been a way of getting noticed.

That being said, think seriously before taking the rebel route. There's no guarantee that it will work. For the first half of my career I defecated in every single audition I went to. Now, there's no way of me knowing for sure that that single thing played a part in my lack of success – but it's fair to say that what worked for Martin Freeman wasn't working for me.

OPINION!
There is NOTHING happening in the Middle East that a good touring Ayckbourn production couldn't solve

If you are set on being a Bad Boy there are many ways of going about it. Invest in a leather jacket. Maybe enter the casting on a jet ski. In the middle of an audition, casually let a used condom fall out of your pocket and say 'What can I say? I love to love'.

Perhaps the greatest of all the rebels was 2002 Colin Farrell. It seems hard to believe but I have it on good authority that he was smoking upwards of ten full-size cigarettes a day at the time. That summer Farrell played Hamlet at the National and the usually 4-hour play lasted 6 hours simply because of all the additional swearing. On paper 'To be or fucking not to be, you know' doesn't look that good but when it came at us via the lips of the majestic Farrell it was just divine. What was truly astonishing was that despite all the extra curse words Farrell's genius was able to recalculate and somehow stay within the iambic pentameter structure.

Ways to be a rebel actor…

1. **Blow smoke in the casting director's face.**

2. **Bring your crack dealer to set.**

3. **Insist on doing all your lines with a rap beat underneath them.**

4. **Walk around with a pit bull at all times, even when acting.**

5. **Never ever be on time – especially for your cues.**

6. **Insist on doing all your own stunts – even if there aren't any in the script.**

7. **Tell everyone that you 'don't do no motherfuckin' warm-ups'. Make sure that you do do one in private though. You're a rebel but you're not reckless.**

8. Stay up past eleven, even when you've got filming in the morning!

9. Walk around with overdue library books and when people ask if you're going to take them back shrug your shoulders.

10. The next time you're self-taping for a casting director – make it look like you're recording it from a prison cell.

TOP TIP!
If you forget a line and someone tries to help you out, shout out 'PAUSE! I WAS DOING A DRAMATIC PAUSE! THEY'RE THE ONE WHO MESSED UP!'

MUSICAL THEATRE

There is no piece of dialogue in the history of theatre or film which could not have been improved by being sung. I always felt that Robert De Niro's 'You talking to me?' in *Taxi Driver* lacked a melody. Or how about 'I'm the King of the world!' from *Titanic*. Surely that would have been better if it had been 'I'm the King. Oh, I'm the King. Yes, I'm the kiiiiiiinggggggg oooooooof theeeeee wooooooooooo ooooooooooooooorld!!!!!'*. Music just has a way of adding class to things. And yet musicals are still sneered upon by the liberal elite who run show business.

That shouldn't stop you wanting to be in one but you must be prepared to work hard. For a character in a musical, singing is a perfectly normal way to express yourself in everyday conversation. The only way to make that convincing is if it becomes the norm for you. For the entire length of the production – from the first day of rehearsal until the last night party is over – it is essential that you sing every single thing that you say. Without that commitment there is always the chance that whilst on stage you will find yourself slipping into normal speech. You owe it to the audience not to take the risk of that happening!

During the production of a musical based on the songs of Roxette, of which I was a proud part of, I do remember this causing me problems from time to time. Fortunately I have very few friends, so on most days my conversational singing was restricted to easy moments to handle like

---

* To hear the melody I am thinking of please buy the as yet uncommissioned audio book.

interactions with bus drivers or supermarket staff. There was one occasion though on which I was tasked with calling up my brother in South Africa and informing him that our mother was dead. Weaker performers, less committed to the craft, might have seen this as a time to make an exception and drop the melody. I was getting paid £120 a week though, I couldn't just abandon my professionalism! Not even for a few seconds.

I am not a monster, so I chose a tune which I thought added an appropriate solemnity to the conversation – Roxette's 'It Must Have Been Love'. It's a gentle ballad with a sad tone. I changed the lyrics of course and told him the terrible news. Unfortunately my brother is ignorant to the practices of the theatre world and so it took at least four verses before he realised that I wasn't joking. It took another fifteen verses for me to explain why I was singing and begin preparations for the funeral.[**]

The constant singing isn't limited to the performers. Most musical directors sing all of their notes and the venue staff are required to sing at all times. I remember once catching a theatre cleaning lady talking *sans* melody and reporting her to the company manager. I'm delighted to say she was immediately fired.

Of course musicals aren't just noted for their singing – there's dancing too! And yes, you can see where I'm going with this – dance as often as you can. Don't walk to the shops. Dance to the shops!

[**] I am disgusted to say that despite traveling 6,000 miles from Cape Town for that funeral, my brother couldn't be bothered to make the further 70-mile journey to see me perform my musical in Northampton.

NUDITY

An actor must always think long and hard before agreeing to do a nude scene.[*] There is always the fear that just a few seconds de-robed could come back to haunt you later in your career. Take Angelina Jolie, Robert De Niro or Helen Mirren. All of them did nude scenes early on in their careers and were never heard of again.

The answer to the question of whether to go nude or not depends on a number of factors, the first of which is… have you been asked to go nude? If neither the script nor the director mention nudity then there is a very real chance that it may not be required. You can't be certain of that though. There are a lot of things people have to think about on a film set and they may have just forgotten to ask you. To be sure, I recommend turning up to the set nude, with your costume in a little bag. That way if they did want nudity, then you're ready to go and if they didn't – no worries – you have your little bag.

Ok, so let's imagine that you've been offered a job and the script does explicitly stipulate that your character is nude at some point. Do you accept the job? Well, that really depends on how comfortable you feel without your clothes on. Walk around your neighbourhood nude for a while. How does it make you feel? Post some videos of yourself in the nude on Facebook. How does that make you feel? If you're ok about it, then great! Call up your

[*]   In fact, thinking 'long and hard' during a nude scene can actually help things, if you know what I mean, but that's another matter.

agent and accept the job. If not, then you should probably turn it down because you wouldn't want to do anything that you'd end up regretting.

For those of you who would accept such a job, there are still some things to think about. We've already established that this could have a detrimental effect on the rest of your career. That's why you should look to capitalise on what could well be your last job as best you can. No more costume means lots more skin and lots more skin means lots more potential advertising space. That's right… tattoos! Companies are always looking for a way to get their name out there. Let's say you're playing one of the naked courtesans in *Game of Thrones*. That's a massive TV show sold all around the world. What an opportunity! Can you imagine how much Goodyear tyres, for example, would be prepared to pay to have their name tattooed across your abdomen? Literally hundreds of pounds! And of course, the more skin you have on show the more companies you can charge to advertise on you. In the run-up to filming you should really be piling on the pounds. Bigger belly equals bigger bucks.

TOP TIP!
Actors have to make people truly believe that they ARE someone else. Practice by trying to get through immigration with a friend's passport

SEX SCENES

If you're nude there's a strong chance it's for what is known in the business as a 'sex scene'. These can be awkward affairs – pretending to make passionate love to someone you hardly know while a crew of fifty people look on.

The only way to make something like that less awkward is through practice. Whenever you have sex with your partner, try to make sure there's a group of people watching. Do it on the beach, at dinner parties, when you have workmen over. Soon it will become second nature. Now, I actually find it difficult to get myself going unless at least fifteen people are looking on.

The practicalities of sex scenes can vary. There is nearly always some degree of simulation taking place. Often the actor places his penis into the vagina of a stunt woman who lies just underneath the actress. Contracts are drawn up so that any children that are born from this process are the property of the studio. This is how a lot of child actors are born.

If the production can't afford a stunt vagina, the actors essentially just

TOP TIP!
Before accepting a romantic role check to see if you have chemistry with the other actor by living with them for a year or so

dry hump each other. This causes problems. We expect our actors to be in character at all times, but at the same time, to avoid embarrassment the male actor is expected to remain unaroused. A little unfair I think. As a courtesy, the actress involved will usually try and limit the likelihood of arousal by letting out a little fart. It's a lovely example of how performers like to look after each other. Manhood subdued, the male actor is allowed to get on with the business of acting.

PORNOGRAPHY

This too often overlooked art form is wall to wall sex scenes and nudity. The actors, and they *are* actors, are very rarely given the credit they deserve. Faking an orgasm as a sweaty Ron Jeremy bears down on you takes training and skill. I challenge Maggie Smith to master it.

There is no reason why these fine actors should be stuck in porn. Making the transition to mainstream acting isn't necessarily as difficult as you might think. Producers are, by nature, filthy. You are far more likely to be seen by one in a low-budget internet porn video than a fringe theatre show. When they return from their industry shindigs, full of Champagne and self-regard, I can guarantee you that they are not googling Brecht. That's why you need to use it as an opportunity to showcase your ability. In the preamble to the action, instead of doing the bog standard sexy small talk, recite a Shakespeare sonnet. Once the sex is in full flow, shout out the usual pleasured expletives but display your versatility by doing each one in a different accent or voice. Their interest should be peaked now. So when it's time for the money shot, whether you're giving or receiving it, get creative and see if you can write out your agent's details with what I sometimes refer to as 'God's ink'.

TOP TIP!
There is a misconception that nudity in fringe theatre is done for shock value. Usually, it's actually just to save on the costume budget

PRE-SHOW ROUTINE

For an actor it is important to have a pre-show routine. Having the stability of a set ritual is a comfort you can't afford to be without before the theatrical hurricane you are about to embark on. Whether it is some odd superstitious tick or just a basic seven-hour warm-up – be sure to have yours down before stepping on stage.

For a 7.30 p.m. evening show I like to get to the theatre at about 7 a.m. just to give myself a chance to get a real sense of the place. Many theatres (particularly regional ones) don't actually open till about 5 p.m. so I'll often spend a lot of time in the car park. A lot of actors become detached from their audiences. It's important for me that I don't – that I remain just a normal guy – so I sit cross-legged in each space for a while and try my best to experience the spiritual environment that my audience will inhabit just before they see me perform. In 2003 I was in a touring production of a failed musical based on the songs of Roxette. I remember one occasion in which I went through this ritual before a show in Chelmsford. Only before it was too late did I realise that I was actually in a car park for Essex County Council's office workers which closed at 6 o'clock. Yes, none of the audience actually used that car park. Do I regret it? No. Absolutely not. I stuck to my routine and my solo in 'Get Dressed For Success' was all the better for it.

Once the theatre is open, this is when the more serious preparation begins. While other actors put on their costumes, having already put mine on before I left the house, I try and boost my confidence by flirting with an usher. If you choose to go down this route I would advise keeping the conversation simple – it is unlikely that the usher will have the same vocabulary as a trained actor. Flick through the programme with them. Explain that the quality of the printing does not do justice to your picture and point out other actors who have less credits than you.

TOP TIP!
If you don't warm up before a performance there is a 40% chance that you will die

Now it's time for a full vocal and body warm-up. I recommend getting yourself in the audience's minds early on by doing this in the theatre bar.

WOMEN!

I can't write this book without devoting roughly a page to one of my favourite types of actor: 'woman actor' or 'actress'. Women have been allowed to act going back as far as the 1960s and I have to say I think they've been a welcome addition to the industry. The first was Julie Andrews who beat George C Scott to the role of Mary Poppins. Although I still think Scott would have done a better job, I have to say Andrews added a special feminine quality to the part.

Today, women are everywhere, taking up to 15% of the leading roles in Hollywood – now that's progress! Some no good do-gooders are still campaigning for a 50/50 split. Look. When women are half of the population, they can have half of the leading roles but until that day – I'm sorry, but… no.

I've heard it said that there aren't enough strong female roles in Hollywood, that it's difficult to find complex interesting women characters who aren't defined by the men in the movie. I disagree. Here are just a few of the sorts of parts an actress in Hollywood can look forward to playing…

Supportive wife of cop.

Concerned mother of teenage boy.

Annoying girlfriend.

Supportive wife of politician.

Sexy woman in bar.

Concerned wife of cop.

Supportive and concerned wife of boxer.

Single girl who can't find the right man.

Woman cheated on by husband.

Kookie friend of woman cheated on by husband.

Sexy woman at sporting event.

Erin Brockovich.

Supportive wife of medieval king.

Kookie friend of supportive wife of medieval king.

Sexy medieval prostitute of medieval king.

**Cate Blanchett-type part
(only to be played by Cate Blanchett).**

Sexy kookie supportive friend of Cate Blanchett part.

So, you see, there really isn't much to complain about.

UNDERSTUDY TIPS

There is a perfectly sensible tradition in the theatre world of having understudies. If, in the normal worlds of the military or medicine or whatever, someone is too sick to go to work – it's not that big of a deal. But how the heck can you do a Wednesday matinee of *A Midsummer Night's Dream* without an Oberon? You can't. And you damn well can't cancel it. That bridge club from Gillingham booked their coach months ago.

An understudy, like the welfare state or always having at least four Cadbury's Trifles in the fridge, is what's known as a safety net. You hope that you don't have to ever use it but it's good to know that it's there. Sweating your guts out for the pleasure of a demanding audience for eighteen hours a week is stressful. Sometimes you need to wind down with a midweek drink and drugs binge. It's far more important that you do that than go to bed at 4 a.m. so that you're capable of making the matinee. As I consistently told the stage manager on the Roxette musical touring show I worked on – *it's for the good of the show*.

Are you an understudy? If the answer is yes then there's something you need to understand. It's not an opportunity to slack off. You should be working *even harder* than the actors who actually have parts. You never know when you could be needed and *what for*. Yes, learn the lines for the parts that you're officially understudying. But what if a company trip to Nando's causes a food poisoning outbreak and the cover for another role goes down as well as the person who's playing it? Then you should be ready to step in. But what if something similar happens at a nearby theatre and there's a chance that the audience of *Jersey Boys* could be turned away? You should be ready to step in. Learn the lines for *all* the parts in *all* the plays on in the city you're working in. It. Is. Your. Duty.

TOP TIP!
The ice cream served in the interval at theatres is usually made from the lead actress's breast milk

As an understudy your goal should always be to get on stage whenever you can. This may mean having to bend the rules a little. If a leading actor happens to trip on something you've 'accidentally' left on some stairs backstage then is that really such a crime? You're not there to sit on your arse and serve their career. You're there to serve your own. If an actor asks if you can give them a cigarette just before the show and you 'accidentally' roll them one containing a healthy dose of crack, it's their fault for being *unprofessional* and smoking before a show.

GREEN ROOM CONVERSATION

There are a select few things it is acceptable to talk about in the green room. Say something wrong or drift into non-permitted territory and you could be blacklisted and banished from the industry forever.

Always be gushingly complimentary about the performance of anyone else in the room. No matter how bad you actually think they are. 'What you're doing is really lovely. You're so talented. I don't know how you do it. You had us all crying back here actually.' That kind of stuff.

Always be heavily critical of anyone who isn't in the room. 'Deborah really needs to pull it together. I don't think she knows her lines, I really don't. I'm sorry but that's what happens when you let people from northern drama schools into the West End. I couldn't understand a word she was saying.' That kind of shit.

People enjoy slagging off other people. Not only does it make them feel better about themselves but it's also lots of fun. If you're the person in the room who does the most slagging off then it stands to reason that you will be the most popular.

Always act like you're really insecure about your own performance. 'Do you honestly think so? I felt like I was just rubbish out there. I really don't know what I'm doing.' Not only is the humble routine enormously likable but it is also a superb way of getting compliments.

If the subject of politics comes up then there is one thing you have to remember at all times – this is a liberal industry. No matter what your actual political opinions are you're going to have to accept that fact. Whatever the topic is, if you want to win the argument and the respect of your colleagues then your goal should be to be the most left-wing person in the room. It is impossible to lose a green room argument by saying something left wing – that is unless someone out left wings you. In the normal world someone may say something like 'Some of my best friends are black'. That might work in the normal world but you don't stand a chance in our world with such a statement. An actor will only impress other actors by saying something like 'All of my friends are black. And gay. And disabled'.

When, in the latter part of the last century, I was between acting jobs for fourteen years I spent some time working in the construction industry. There the rules on political conversation are reversed. If you ever end up in a similar situation your aim should be to be the most right-wing person on the building site. You must be anti-immigration, pro-monarchy and anti-diving in football. For actors of course it's pro-immigration, anti-monarchy and pro-diving in football – because we appreciate the acting ability it takes.

Much of this advice applies to your behaviour not only in the green room but also on Facebook, by the way. The eyes of the industry are watching everything you do. Don't, for heaven's sake, put a foot wrong. If you saw a friend in a show, make sure you write a status saying how 'incredible' they were. But write it *during* the show. That way, you'll look like a nice supportive actor but we'll all know that *really* they weren't very good and you should have got the fucking job instead.

TOP TIP!
If a line in the script is in italics that means you should be leaning when you say it

DANIEL DAY-LEWIS FACTS

1. Daniel Day-Lewis dreams in character.

2. Daniel Day-Lewis has a medical degree just in case he ever plays a doctor.

3. Daniel Day-Lewis has three lungs which gives him greater vocal capacity.

4. Daniel Day-Lewis can change height to suit his character's status in the scene.

5. Whilst being a cow during animal work at drama school, Daniel Day-Lewis developed four stomachs.

6. Daniel Day-Lewis is able to sense when an actor within a 200-mile radius is giving a bad performance.

7. Daniel Day-Lewis turned down the role of Superman because he couldn't actually fly.

8. At the age of eight Daniel Day-Lewis got down to the last two to play Vito Corleone in *The Godfather*.

9. When not working, Daniel Day-Lewis lives in the forest and talks exclusively to the ghosts of great actors from the past as these are the only people he can relate to.

10. Daniel Day-Lewis had sex with your mother as research for a role.

11. Daniel Day-Lewis is a mute, who can only talk when acting.

12. If another actor makes a mistake, Daniel Day-Lewis kills and eats them.

13. In 1984 Daniel Day-Lewis spent two months working as a Santa in a shopping mall. To prepare he put on 90 pounds and spent two months living in Lapland.

14. Daniel Day-Lewis was once so 'in character' that he managed to change blood type.

15. A great actor can go up to half an hour without breathing when pretending to be dead onstage. Daniel Day-Lewis can go for three days.

ENTRANCES

Acting, like anything else in life, is about making a good first impression. This is why entrances are so important. It doesn't matter how good your performance is if you stumble onto stage like an amateur. Here are some tips...

<u>BE PROMPT</u>

Here, I go with the dictum: 'tis better to be early than late. That's why I recommend making all your entrances at least four lines early. An added advantage to this is that all the other actors will be thrown by your arrival. Their performances will no doubt suffer – making you look better by comparison.

<u>BE SPECTACULAR</u>

Your intention should be to be transfixing from the second you're on stage. It is my belief that many a Chekhov production could be vastly improved by spending some of the rehearsal process workshopping with Cirque du Soleil. Think how much more entertaining *Three Sisters* would be if each of the sisters entered by leaping through a ring of fire.

BE DIFFERENT

Let's say you're in a production of *The Merchant of Venice*, your first entrance is in the second act and the cast are all in Elizabethan dress. Who are the audience expecting to see enter the stage? Another character in the same old Jacobean garb. Who are they not expecting to see? A man wearing shorts and a Fat Willy's Surf Shack T-shirt.

BE LOUD

Always grab the audience's attention by screaming your first line in a loud, disconcerting falsetto shriek. Let them know you're there! Once they do – you can go into whatever voice you and the director have agreed on.

BE SEXY

One of the most memorable entrances in movie history came from Cameron Diaz in *The Mask*. The camera starts on a lady's hands doing up the strap on a sexy high heel. We then pan up to see her incredible curves and land on her stunning face. She shakes her head, showing off her beautiful blonde locks. Sultry sax plays and she confidently struts towards our protagonist. There is no reason why that exact same entrance couldn't work for you when you get your first professional acting role – a paramedic with two lines on *Holby City*. Just arrive on set, tell the crew what you want and make it happen.

BE SURPRISING

A trick regularly used in modern, experimental or, as it's more commonly known, 'turgid' theatre is to plant an actor in the audience and have them make their first entrance from there. The punters love it. As they travel home to their boring little civilian families they exclaim 'Can you believe it Brenda? I, Martin, an insurance broker from East Grinstead, was sat next to a real-life actual actor and I didn't even know it!'. I like to go one step further. In those instances the shock gradually subsides as the actor is assimilated into the action on stage. But what if the cast themselves don't even know you're making an entrance? That's why I like to attend plays simply as a punter and when I feel the play is getting dull – stand up and shout random lines at the actors. Do it! Not only will your entrance be unexpected by the audience. It is also a complete surprise to the cast and venue staff. As you are removed from the theatre be sure to have some résumés to hand out to any casting directors that might be in.

TOP TIP!
If the director gives you a critical note throw your head back, laugh and say 'ABSOLUTELY!'. This shows you're comfortable with critique.

WHAT AN ACTOR
SPENDS THEIR MONEY ON...

■ **12.00%** | Essentials - bills, rent, food, lubricant, etc.

■ **15.00%** | Bank charges.

■ **31%** | Pinot Grigio.

■ **42%** | Redoing head shots.

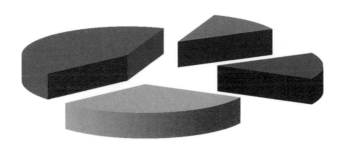

EXTREME ACTING TIPS

There may come a point in your career where you feel that acting doesn't provide you with the same kind of buzz it used to. In your early years, just walking on as a servant and placing a tray of tea on a table was enough to keep you creatively stimulated for weeks. Now, even a dramatic scene in which you confront your father about how he abused you as a child won't do it for you. Perhaps it even bores you.

If this sounds familiar then the chances are that you have 'actor's fatigue'. I've seen many an actor crippled by this horrible affliction – unable to motivate themselves to read even a sonnet. These poor victims sit at home not even caring if their agent rings and doing things which are completely alien to an actor like washing their car or even DIY.

There is a cure though. It's not an easy one and it doesn't come without its risks but I can guarantee that it will make acting get your pulse racing once again. It's called… extreme acting.

The idea is that you put yourself into situations in which you have literally no other choice than to act. The higher the stakes are, the bigger the thrill. Here's my favourite extreme acting game…

TRIAL

This takes a lot of planning and should you fail in your goal, the price you pay will be enormous. The idea is that you get yourself on trial for murder and then try and 'act' your way out of it.

The first thing you're going to need to do is frame yourself. *I do not condone actually murdering someone for this game.* Maybe get a job at an old people's home and start mentioning to the other staff that you've been changing wills and 'helping' people into the afterlife. Whatever works for you. The key thing is to get yourself a conviction.

Your appearance on the stand will be the greatest test your acting ability will ever face. Ideally you will have done such a good job of framing yourself that the challenge will be immense. All you should have to help you convince that jury that you are innocent are your skills of deception. But, I imagine you're saying, I could always just tell them that I framed myself. Think about it. Only someone truly insane would do such a thing. A jury would never believe that an actor would do something like that just for the thrill of it. Only an actor knows how far they'll go for their craft. You'll be on your own. Good luck!

FRUGAL LIVING TIPS

Based on a survey I did of me and two friends, the average actor earns about £3500 a year. It's not easy to live off such a small amount of money. Here are some tips on getting by...

1. **Walk everywhere. Not only does this save on money but it also allows you to arrive at auditions already warmed up. The sweat that will be pouring off you says to the director, 'I'm a hard worker'.**

2. **Never buy toilet paper. Instead, do all your dirty work at auditions. If you don't get an audition for a while – go to your agent's office. If you don't have an agent – do it at home but use pages from Spotlight. I take particular pleasure in soiling actresses who've turned down my advances or actors who've beaten me to jobs.**

3. **Find food where you can. If the receptionist at an audition has a bowl of sweets on her desk – pour them all into your bag when they're looking the other way.**

4. **Another place you can get free food is at Sikh temples. Thanks to the generosity of the Sikh religion, you will usually find more actors at your average Sikh temple than actual Sikhs.**

5. Live with your parents. This will save you money but also give you the angst which is required to be a good actor.

6. Instead of forking out for a photographer – draw a picture of yourself for your headshot.

7. If you still can't afford the Spotlight entry fee – forget head shots altogether. Just make sure your face is always in casting director's heads by appearing to them as a ghost at some point.

8. Steal an item of costume from every job you do. My wardrobe spans many centuries of fashion.

9. Steal a prop from every job you do. I brush my teeth with a broom I got from the set of a play I did thirteen years ago.

10. Save money on tax and agent's commission by never getting any work.

TOP TIP!
Street theatre is a great way to earn extra cash but don't jump in at the deep end. Start with Cul-de-sac theatre and work your way up

CV TIPS

A CV or 'résumé' is a tangible document from which someone can assess just how successful your acting career has been thus far. You may give the best audition Soho has ever seen but if your résumé only has a couple of drama school productions and a walk-on part in *Heartbeat* on it you don't stand a chance.

First and foremost you need to appear to have as many credits as possible. The truth is irrelevant. These days casting directors are so busy that they frequently don't even bother to look at the CVs. They determine how many credits you have by weighing them. A simple way to cheat here is by using a much larger font.

Another way of disguising an unimpressive CV is by printing it in Braille. Political correctness will make them feel too awkward to ask for a proper one.

You can't count on them not looking at it though so if you don't have many real credits you're going to need to conjure up some artificial ones. Here are seven methods...

1. **Include not just everything you've been in but also everything you've seen.**

2. **Fabricate a Bollywood career. They'll never bother to check whether it exists.**

3. **Include school plays.**

4. **List it not by production you've been in but by scene you were in or even by line you've said.**

5. **Say you were in something on BBC4. No one actually watches that so they won't know.**

6. **List shit jobs you've had in such a way that they look like acting work… e.g. If you've worked in an office say you were in *The Office*.**

7. **List unsuccessful auditions. If you took the time to work on something you should get credit for it.**

Your CV isn't just about credits, there's a skills section too. Many people make the basic error of forgetting to list the most important skill of all… 'acting'. In Britain all CVs go on a website run by a company called Spotlight. Spotlight helpfully give you a list of skills you might like to add. Tick every box. EVERY ONE. It doesn't matter if you can't actually ride a horse. If you fail to perform on the day they can easily sort it out in post-production. TICK EVERY BOX. You never know what skill could get you a job. In forty years' time when you get the job of playing Indonesia's most famous sportsman you'll be glad you ticked 'highly skilled at badminton'.

TOP TIP!
An award-winning actor just has to have an award. It doesn't have to be for acting. Awards for swimming, for example, count

TAX TIPS

The fact that actors have to pay tax is a disgrace and everyone knows it. I have been sat here for a good six or seven minutes now and I can't think of a single profession that does more for the world. A doctor can heal you, yes. But thanks to the research they will have done, an actor who has *played* a doctor can heal you too, but in a far more entertaining way.

While the powers that be continue to tax us, we will continue to fight them with the only weapon we've got – expenses. Here is a list of things you can and should claim for…

ALL PHONE BILLS

It's not just calls to your agent which are deductible. Any conversation you have can be viewed as a voice exercise.

ALL FOOD

Without the vital nourishment provided to us by food, actors wouldn't be able to do what they do. Write it down as 'actors' fuel'.

HOLIDAYS

Actors sometimes work up to 20 hours a week. Without a rest now and again our skills would be diminished. Any vacation can count as a research trip too. You went to Italy in case you were ever cast in *The Two Gentlemen of Verona*. You went to Australia in case you were ever cast in *Neighbours*. You went to Jamaica in case you were ever cast in a Lilt advert.

COCAINE

It takes confidence to step on a stage. Cocaine gives us that.

PROSTITUTES

Like with anything else, when it comes to sex scenes – practice makes perfect.

TOP TIP!
To prove you are a self-employed actor the tax office will want to see a classical and a modern audition piece

Oh, Shakespeare. Just hearing his name is, for me, like stepping into a lovely warm bath. There is not a single one of his plays which I do not love passionately and return to on a weekly basis. *Hamlet*, *As You Like It*, *Oliver Twist*. They're all delightful in their own special ways. We all remember the first time we heard Shakespeare at school and *immediately* loved it. Here's something from *Henry IV: Part I*…

> *'As the honey of Hybla, my old lad of the castle – and is not a buff jerkin a most sweet robe of durance?'*

Now, that line just speaks to me. I read it and I immediately knew exactly what he was talking about. Isn't it about time someone said that about buff jerkins? They *are* in a most sweet robe of durance. All the bloody time! Only Shakespeare would have the balls to speak the truth to jerkins. And not just any jerkins. *Buff* jerkins at that. Quite incredible.

TOP TIP!
Go to a Shakespeare production and laugh loudly and knowingly in random places. This will show you 'get it'

I've heard it said that Shakespeare can be incomprehensible but that is just absurd. If you don't understand Shakespeare the second that you read it for the first time then you have no right to call yourself an actor.

It is true that much of the language he used has fallen out of fashion. This upsets me and I try to keep it alive myself by using it whenever I can. In everyday conversation I will often throw a 'doth' or a 'privy' into the odd sentence, just to impress people. It always works.

If you are currently working on a Shakespeare production then you should be using that kind of language all the time. In fact, I would go so far as to say that all of your conversations should be in iambic pentameter. If you're truly in character then that really shouldn't be too difficult. Think about it. In Elizabethan times *everyone* spoke in iambic pentameter *all the time* so why should it be so hard for you to do?

So what is it about Shakespeare that has stood the test of time? Well, for a start he's still as funny as he ever was. The jesters are always hilarious! Take this speech from the Fool in *King Lear*…

> *'Why – after I have cut the egg i' th' middle and eat up the meat – the two crowns of the egg. When thou clovest thy crown i' th' middle, and gavest away both parts, thou borest thy ass o' th' back o'er the dirt. Thou hadst little wit in thy bald crown when thou gavest thy golden one away.'*

You can't help but laugh can you? It's brilliant! I challenge any of the modern 'comedians' to come up with something anywhere near as amusing as that.

Perhaps my favourite comic character is Thersites, the fool from *Troilus and Cressida*. Here's one of his particularly chuckle-inducing gags…

'O! thou great thunder-darter of Olympus, forget that thou art Jove, the king of gods, and, Mercury, lose all the serpentine craft of thy caduceus, if ye take not that little, little less than little wit from them that they have; which short-armed ignorance itself knows is so abundant scarce, it will not in circumvention deliver a fly from a spider, without drawing their massy irons and cutting the web.'

The guy is a riot! That's as funny as anything Will Ferrell has ever said, I can tell you that for a start. If you are ever fortunate enough to play Thersites my advice would be this: don't worry about adding anything to *make* it funny. No silly voices, no funny little tricks. That kind of comedy magma doesn't need such nonsense. Just walk on stage, say those lines, and wait for the laughs to roll in.

TOP TIP!
In a period drama? Show you're truly in character by freaking out at the lighting, microphones and cameras

It is fair to say that in this modern world of Sega Game Gears and cress heads, Shakespeare can struggle to hold the attention of today's youth. Their minds are so polluted with the notion that Shakespeare isn't for them – probably an idea spread by Lil Wayne or whoever – that it's difficult to get them to even listen.

When performing to a young audience I accept that some concessions need to be made to arouse them. Take Antony's famous speech from *Julius Caesar*.

> 'Friends, Romans, countrymen, lend me your ears;
> I come to bury Caesar, not to praise him.'

To a modern, no doubt pregnant fifteen-year-old with a history of glue sniffing, those words mean nothing. Let's try and prick their interest...

> 'Friends, Romans, countrymen, lend me your ears yeah?
> Listen right, I come to bury Caesar, not to praise him yeah?'

The original text hasn't been damaged at all but you'll find any youngsters in your audience are paying closer attention now. To get them really on board you may need to spice things up a little further...

> 'Friends, Romans, fucking countrymen, lend me your fucking ears yeah?
> Just fucking listen right, I come to bury this prick Caesar, not to fucking praise him yeah?'

Suddenly that large school group is hanging on your every word and none of the beauty of the original verse has been lost. Without even knowing it they're learning about the majesty of Shakespeare's language.

TOP TIP!
Shakespeare didn't write ANY of his 200 plays on a computer. Not one!

WHAT ACTORS WHO SAY THEY'VE 'BEEN BUSY' HAVE ACTUALLY BEEN DOING...

0.01% | Film work.

2% | TV.

7% | Profit share theatre above a pub.

11% | Being a skeleton at the London Dungeon.

81% | Handing out flyers for nightclubs on stilts.

STAGE NAME

An actor's stage name is vitally important. There's no getting away from the fact that when people are considering you for a role, your name will have a subconscious effect on the way they see you. Exploit that fact! A name that doesn't say anything about you and your skills is redundant. Here are some names that are definitely not…

Martin Available

Sharon Versatile

Little Jimmy Odd Face

Trevor Experienced

Sarah Accomplished

Scott Comedy

Deborah Famous

Steven Stage-Fighter

Elizabeth Sober-Now

Philip Fat

Stephanie French-Speaker

Andrew Accents

Hannah Husky

Todd Sings

Spontaneous Bone

Benedict Cumberbatchofgoodcredits

TELLING YOUR PARENTS

It's hard to believe in this day and age but there are still many people too scared to tell their parents that they are an actor. If you are fortunate enough to be born in a modern liberal city like London or Los Angeles then your parents will probably be sufficiently open-minded to tolerate, perhaps even celebrate who you are. Tragically though, there are still people being born every day outside a twenty-mile radius of a Wholefoods.

Should you come from such a backwater then you will need to think very carefully about if, when and how you tell your parents the full truth about yourself. It may well be that your parents already have suspicions. Think about it. If you still live with them have you left any telling clues around the house? Plays? The odd stray codpiece? This book?

TOP TIP!
Test your skills of believability by trying to convince your parents that your acting career is 'actually going quite well'

It could well be that your behaviour has already got them wondering. Maybe you're particularly good at lying. Maybe you've recently started collecting comedy and tragedy masks. Perhaps your favourite Attenborough is Richard. These are all odd things which are unlikely to have gone without notice.

It's one thing for them to ponder the thought that you could be an actor. It's another thing to hear those words come from your mouth though.

'Mum. Dad. I am an actor.'

However well enunciated and projected those words are (they will be: you're an actor) they are likely to make your parents physically sick. The first thing they will do is wonder what they did wrong. 'We should never have taken them to see that pantomime when they were five!'. 'Why oh why oh why did we let them appear in that nativity?'. 'I told you no one normal actually *listens* to CDs of musicals!'.

Explain to them that there's nothing they could have done differently. The fact is, you were born an actor. It's in your genes. If needs be, take a blood test and show it to them to prove it.

Then their worries will come out. Do your best to reassure them.

'Aren't their lots of diseases you can get?'

Tell them yes, kissing scenes do spread germs, but there are precautions you can take. Echinacea. Hot water, honey and lemon. Explain that if you do catch one, Dr. Theatre will treat it.

'I don't want you to be an outcast.'

Tell them that acting is becoming more and more acceptable. They even allow it to be shown on television these days!

'Does this mean you won't be able to give us grandchildren?'

Of course you will. And not just any grandchildren. If things go well you'll be able to do an Angelina Jolie and buy extra specially beautiful grandchildren from the Third World.

TOP TIP!
Does your child want to be an actor when they grow up? If so – torture them. They will need the painful memories to draw on in later life

THE OSCARS

THE RED CARPET

Success in acting goes hand in hand with red carpets. The only other profession which features red carpets quite so heavily is '1980s pimp'. The reason behind Hollywood's persistent use of them is little known.

Did you know that when an A-list actor walks down a red carpet they are actually performing a kind of victory dance? Well, they are. The colour red represents all the metaphorical blood shed by the actors who failed to get big parts in movies. When an A-lister walks down the red carpet they are effectively walking all over that blood. It's their way of asserting power over those who are still behind them in the industry. They want to keep you down. It's a sickening ritual but, if you ever get the chance to do it, enormous fun!

The first thing you need to think about is your arrival. The moment you step out of the limo, the eyes of the world's press are going to be on you so your entrance has to be right. I'm yet to see someone fire themselves out of the sun roof from

TOP TIP!
Without a BTEC in Performing Arts you are going to find it very difficult to break into Hollywood and that is just a fact

the ejector seat. Why not be the first? It's a good way of putting yourself in the frame for action movies, particularly if you're normally typecast in a different kind of role. Meryl Streep, for example, could really benefit from such an entrance.

You could of course dispense with the limo altogether and arrive on a bicycle. This says that you're actually really casual about these sort of things. It says 'I mean, yeah, I'm really happy for everyone and it will be great to see some of my buddies and have you any idea what the stuff we're pumping into the atmosphere is doing to our planet and, you know, for me it's all about the work and I'm not really concerned with collecting trophies because I'm an artist'. That kind of shit. Very marketable. If you do go with the bicycle entrance, make sure you continue to wear your fluorescent clothing throughout the evening. That way once you're in the venue, you'll be immediately recognisable in any wide shots.

Once you're on the red carpet it's all about the interview with E! A good indicator of just how far you've come in your career is whether you are asked to speak with Ryan Seacrest or Giuliana Rancic. A chat with Seacrest says 'We think you're going to be a star for a while,' whereas a chat with Rancic says 'Look. Well done for writing the music for this Polish film and everything but do you really think you're going to be here next year?'. Although undoubtedly better for your career, the Seacrest interview doesn't come without a price. Ryan may seem like the innocent little boy who fell into the botox factory but he is in fact a ruthless parasitic reptile who feeds off of all who stand before him. You will not be allowed to leave until he has symbolically eaten something representing a part of your soul. Some will just give him a trinket from their handbag, the more ambitious might let him eat one of their fingers. Anne Hathaway has gone through six hands.[*]

No matter who you end up talking to the first question will always be the same: 'Who are you wearing?'. It used to be 'What are you wearing?' but the producers decided that the answers 'a suit' and 'a dress' were becoming boring. The frustrating thing with the 'who?' question is that you're there to promote yourself and yet the first thing you end up doing is promoting someone else. To avoid this pitfall I recommend making your own clothes. Even if your skills in this area are poor and you end up wearing a glorified bath mat, at least when the question comes you will be able to answer with your own name and get vital extra publicity. *Trust* me on this.

Many actors find the obsession with their outfits a little silly and prefer to talk about their work. A good way of bypassing the fashion conversation altogether is to arrive naked. That way, you and the interviewer are able to forget

---

[*]   My publisher has asked me to make it clear that this is all speculation. Living in the UK means that I watch most red carpet at 1 a.m. in a Tia Maria and Cadbury's mini roll induced haze. I concede that that may have influenced the way I see the broadcast. I like to go with motto – if you have a potentially libellous theory you're not entirely sure about, write it down, print it in a book and see how you feel about it in a couple of years.

any petty distractions and have a serious conversation about 'the craft'.

If you insist on wearing clothes, think long and hard about what will get you noticed. The following day all the papers will do a 'best and worst dressed' feature. Everyone is trying to get into the 'best dressed' section which means that it's harder to do. The chances are that in aiming for it, you'll fall just short and miss out on being pictured altogether. Go all out for the 'worst dressed' category. If you're the only person who's actually gunning for that then you're pretty much guaranteed to get in. Wearing a wet suit should do it.

Once the fashion has been dealt with they will most likely ask you if it was fun to work with your co-stars. Most actors go for a polite variation on 'Yes, it was incredible. Leo (or whoever) is such a generous actor'. This, I feel, is a little short-sighted. Your co-star on one movie could easily soon be your competition for another role. With the way the liberal elite and their filthy agenda control Hollywood, this could even be true if you're different genders. Complimenting them only aides their career and not yours. Instead, use this as an opportunity to spread damaging gossip about them…

'Working with Leo was quite difficult actually. It's hard playing opposite someone who's more interested in his bloody Tamagotchi than the movie he's supposed to be working on.'

THE CEREMONY

I have never actually been to an awards ceremony. The closest I ever got was a prize giving at school at which I'm proud to say I won a commendation for my felt work in textiles class. Our event lasted just an hour because we were squeezed between the after school badminton club and a lady's self-defence class which was booked into the sports hall at 7 p.m., but I'm told that Hollywood ceremonies can go on for as long as five hours. That is because in an effort to appear nice they give awards for ridiculous things. Cinematography! I mean, come on! You can't make a movie without actors but you sure can make one without cameras. It just has to be a sort of 'live movie' or as it's otherwise referred to, a 'play'. The list of pointless awards is endless. Costume! Visual Effects! Editing! No one even knows what these things are. *Sound* mixing! What the fuck is that? As an actor the extensive work I have done on my vocal chords and diaphragm means I can do all my sound mixing myself, thank you very much.

TOP TIP!
When acting in a film it's important to silently hum the soundtrack in your head

The ceremony should be a simple two hours long. Best Actress, Best Actor, Best Supporting Actor, Best Supporting Actress. A half-hour speech for each and then we'd be done. But, no. We have to hang around for 'Foreign Language Film', which I am appalled to note, is never won by an English-speaking film – which *is* a foreign language to the majority of the world. It's outright racism!

As a nominated actor, the whole evening will have been leading up to one moment for you – the goodie bag. This is an entirely appropriate custom. There is no job on earth more stressful than Hollywood actor. A small bag containing little things like Rolex watches and free vouchers for luxury spa retreats is just a way of making a small dent in the pain they go through to entertain the ungrateful masses.

There is of course another big moment for a nominated actor – the opening of the envelope. Actors have long been judged for their ability to look pleased for the winner when they miss out. I would argue that it's not actually necessary. Seeing as everyone smiles for each other, it's not a great way of getting noticed. Instead, throw a Kanye West-style tantrum. Earn the respect of your peers by showing how much the award meant to you as you run on stage and wrestle it from Reese Witherspoon's hands.

THE SPEECH

If you have read this book thoroughly and taken it in properly there will come a point when you will have to make an Oscars acceptance speech. So many actors mess this up. It's the biggest moment of their careers and yet they waste it crying and thanking their families. This is down to a lack of preparation and that most overvalued

Hollywood commodity – humility. You've just won a fucking Oscar for crying out loud. This is not a time to be humble. This is a time to settle scores.

Thanks to a run-in I had with the Church of Scientology last year, it now looks like I will never win an Oscar myself. What pains me most about this is that the world will never get to see the acceptance speech I have slaved over for many years. Should you wish to use it yourself, please, be my guest...

> *'Wow! Well... oh boy! Wow! Thank you so much. Fuck you Steven Gibbs! Fuck you! Thanks guys. Thank you so much. Look at me now Steven Gibbs you little prick! Thank you. Hey Steven! You used to laugh at my shoes at school and gave me a dead arm on no less than three occasions but look at me now! I'm officially the best actor in the whole fucking world and what are you Steve? What are you? Seriously? You don't seem to be on Facebook so I don't actually know. But unless you got a fucking nose job and changed your name to Jared Leto I'm pretty sure you haven't got one of these little puppies. Thank you all so much.*
>
> *I'd like to start by thanking the Academy, which let's face it, we all know is code for the Illuminati. Am I right guys?! I would thank the director and the crew and that but everyone knows that the camera was pointed at me and not them for a reason.*

To everyone who ever turned me down for a job I want you to know that you only gave me the drive to succeed. So to the casting directors at the RSC, the BBC, every West End theatre and those in charge of casting commercials for KFC, moneysupermarket. com, Lenor, Persil, some Dutch Insurance company, P&O Cruises, Chocco Shreddies, Wonga.com and the No!No! Hair Removal System – I DON'T NEED YOU NOW! I've won an Oscar. I've made it! People don't win an Oscar and then just disappear. They stay famous and rich forever! Yes, I haven't seen Mo'Nique in much since she won supporting for Precious *but I'm sure she's still working.*

INTERESTING FACT!
If you want it enough you WILL one day win an Oscar. That's just basic mathematics

So here I am. An Oscar winner. I've got to say it feels great. It was a pretty good performance though wasn't it? If you thought that clip was good, you should have been there on the day… electric! For those of you who haven't seen the film yet, my best bit was probably when I… wait, I'll show you…

THEN DO A SCENE FROM FILM. IT SHOULD BE NO MORE THEN TWELVE

MINUTES LONG. THERE'S NO NEED TO MILK IT.

Good wasn't it? So, I did some research and apparently I don't actually get any money for this which I have to say strikes me as bullshit. Anyway, listen, I'll see you at the after parties yeah? And to anyone who's won a pissy little Oscar for Best Documentary Short or something, don't be thinking you can be stealing my thunder on the dance floor tonight. I've made my own playlist and everything. Alright. Peace out.'

THE END

Well, here we are. The end. Just take a moment to think about the person you were when you started this book, some ninety minutes ago. You knew nothing. You were a headless chicken floundering in a business that didn't love you and that you didn't understand.

But now look at yourself. Go over to a mirror and have a good look at yourself. You're a real actor. Congratulations! You've absorbed the wisdom within and you've changed for the better. You're welcome.

But your journey is not over. Actors are forever learning. Now is not the time to rest on your laurels. I want you to immediately read the book again. Bear in mind though that you've already extracted most of the knowledge from this particular copy, so you will need to buy another.

One more thing. It has been pointed out to me that some of the tips in this book contradict each other. That is because I wrote the bulk of it on an overnight Megabus journey after a bad audition in Edinburgh. My head wasn't in the right place.

TOP TIP!
The first rule of acting
is to ALWAYS be
yourself

Fergus Craig is an actor who has performed at the Young Vic and the RSC and been a regular on a number of TV shows including *Anna and Katy* (Channel 4), *Star Stories* (Channel 4), *Sorry I've Got No Head* (CBBC) and *Popatron* (BBC2). He has written for *Cardinal Burns* (Channel 4), *Anna and Katy*, *Sorry I've Got No Head* and many BBC Radio shows including *Colin and Fergus's Digi Radio*. At the time of writing, he has never appeared in a musical based on the songs of Roxette.

WWW.OBERONBOOKS.COM

Follow us on www.twitter.com/@oberonbooks
& www.facebook.com/oberonbook